Coordinating
Human Services

New Strategies for Building

Service Delivery Systems

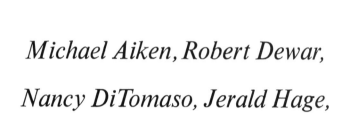

Michael Aiken, Robert Dewar,

Nancy DiTomaso, Jerald Hage,

Gerald Zeitz

COORDINATING

HUMAN

SERVICES

Jossey-Bass Publishers
San Francisco · Washington · London · 1975

COORDINATING HUMAN SERVICES
New Strategies for Building Service Delivery Systems
by Michael Aiken, Robert Dewar, Nancy DiTomaso,
Jerald Hage, and Gerald Zeitz

The Jossey-Bass

Behavioral Science Series

Preface

Between October 1963 and October 1965, the Vocational Rehabilitation Administration (now Social and Rehabilitation Services) of the Department of Health, Education, and Welfare funded five research and demonstration projects whose purpose was to bring about coordination of services for the mentally retarded in five different metropolitan areas: Milwaukee, San Francisco, Cleveland, Los Angeles, and Bridgeport, Connecticut. For each of these projects, a different type of agency or organization received the five-year grant. In one instance, funds went to a parents group; in another, a private service delivery organization received the grant; in the third, a voluntary association of professionals was the recipient; in the fourth, a traditional United Fund welfare federation was the key agency; and in the fifth, a specially created organization emerged from a formal joint-powers contract between the city, county, and state governments. Furthermore, each of these projects was distinctive in its approach to the problem and in its organizing techniques and procedures.

In our analysis of these projects (described in Chapters

Two through Six), we focus on their attempts to make changes in the basic distribution of resources for the retarded—that is, their attempts at community organization and action. We view the organizations that contracted for the grants in each community as change agents that intervened in the service delivery of each community in an attempt to bring about coordination of programs and services, resources, clients, and information. Hence, we are interested in their goals, what they attempted to do; in their power bases, the resources they directly controlled; in their strategies, how they attempted to bring about change; in their intervention points, the places within the system where action was first attempted; and in their links, their relationships with other agencies or groups. In addition, in Chapter One we define and discuss the concept of coordination and point out various institutional barriers to successful coordination. We also describe the various stages through which a change process (specifically, the creation of a coordinated service delivery system) must proceed.

After these five projects were completed or nearing completion, we were commissioned by the funding agency, Social and Rehabilitation Services, to study them—particularly their effectiveness in improving the delivery of rehabilitation services. We gathered the data for this study in part through unstructured intensive interviews with knowledgeable informants and in part through examination of the extensive documents produced by the five projects. The interviews were conducted by us between 1968 and 1971, either near the end of the particular project or shortly after its completion. Each project was assigned as the primary responsibility of one of us, though some were conducted by teams of two, and each community was visited by at least two and sometimes by four of us. The number of interviews varied in each community, the exact number depending on the size of the project (the larger the project, the more interviews) and the availability of documents (the more documents, the fewer the interviews). In general, we used a "snowball" method of selecting respondents, starting with the two or three key participants in each community and acquiring names of other people less centrally involved. In addition to this

snowball method, we made efforts to interview those with conflicting views and conclusions about the projects.

Moreover, given the great differences among these projects and the many unique factors of each, we approached them
to some extent as five case studies, even though as sociologists
we had a basic interest in extracting general principles. We did,
of course, generate some general principles and hypotheses that
we feel are supported by the evidence of these projects; these
generalizations are discussed in the final two chapters of the
book.

A further reason for our using a relatively unstructured
and open-ended approach was the lack of specific hypotheses to
test. Few studies have been made of service delivery systems—
how to create them, how they operate, and how to improve
efficiency in them. Since the projects were conceived by many
of the participants as attempts at interorganizational cooperation, we initially examined the interorganizational literature
(for example, Aiken and Hage, 1968; Evan, 1966; H. E. Aldrich,
1971; Litwak and Meyer, 1970) in some detail. We found this
literature only partly applicable since it ignored matters of community power, state and national politics, and the like, which
were as important in explaining the outcomes of these projects
as organizational or interorganizational factors.

The concept of a service delivery system is relatively new
and therefore has not been studied or explained in any detail.
Such a system is part community subsystem, part interorganizational set, and part rationalized bureaucracy. However, it does
not exactly fit into any of these categories; therefore, the literature on community, community organization, interorganizational relations, and organizational behavior is not completely
sufficient to encompass our concerns here. We feel that our
open-ended procedures to some extent allowed us to explore
broadly the factors involved in these attempts to coordinate
services for the mentally retarded; as a result, we have emerged
with some insights about service delivery systems in general.

The introductory and concluding chapters (One, Seven,
Eight) were developed through innumerable discussions among
us. We discussed, outlined, drafted, redrafted, edited, and

omitted at many points along the way. Thus, this book is a collective product in the full sense of the word. Chapters Two
through Six were each the primary responsibility of one author,
who did the research, but these too were edited and revised by
all of us. Nancy DiTomaso is primarily responsible for Chapter
Two; Jerald Hage for Chapters Three and Five; Robert Dewar
for Chapter Four; and Gerald Zeitz for Chapter Six. Michael
Aiken oversaw and participated in the data collection for San
Francisco, Milwaukee, and Cleveland, and also wrote the original version of the introductory and concluding chapters based
on our collective discussions. Hage wrote a second draft of the
introduction and conclusion, which were then substantially
revised. The final versions of Chapters One, Seven, and Eight
grew out of extensive discussion by the five of us. Although
these chapters are collaborative, some sections reflect the work
of one person more than others. In Chapter One, Aiken is responsible for writing the extended discussion of coordination
based on the conversations of the five of us and for the discussions on multiple local governments. Hage is responsible for the
rest of the material on institutional barriers and primarily for
Chapter Eight. Chapter Seven is a collaborative effort; each
author contributed to various parts of it. Therefore, the order
of names on the book is alphabetical and in no way implies anything more than equal responsibility.

Chapters One, Seven, and Eight represent a series of compromises among us as we attempted to forge a coherent and
unified synthesis of the meaning of this research experience.
Differences in intellectual orientation and style led to some significant disagreements over emphasis on different ideas. For
example, there was the dilemma of whether to argue for one
"best" solution to the problem of coordination or to discuss the
advantages and disadvantages of various alternatives, without
necessarily making a definite choice among them. Our political
and intellectual persuasions, ranging from pluralism to reform
pluralism to more left and radical orientations, resulted in different preferences for particular solutions and different percep-
tions of the underlying causes of problems. Specifically, some

of us prefer the solution of integration of all services for all clients into a common service delivery system. Others believe that a decentralized system, as represented by a coalition of organizations, is the best arrangement for service delivery in the foreseeable future. Implicit in each of these views are different assessments of the implications of these various solutions for power distribution, innovation, and conflict. Some of us feel that a totally integrated system would not be sufficiently powerful to generate adequate resources, that conflict would not be creatively channeled in a centralized arrangement, and that innovation would be unlikely; others of us have the opposite opinion. Some of us believe that a coalition of agencies would be more successful in generating funding and that implementation of new services is more likely in a competitive system; others of us think conflict in a coalition might be too great and unproductive. There are no easy answers, but the questions are clearly able to be tested, and we hope they will be the focus of future research.

We do essentially agree that integration of case management in public agencies would go a long way toward solving many of the problems presently confronting most multiproblem clients. We also agree that the issue of coordination is an exceedingly complex one, and we hope that one of the major contributions of this effort is to make clear what is involved when coordination is being discussed and advocated. We agree too that the strategies for creating coordination are as complex as the concept itself.

Although Social and Rehabilitation Services provided the financial support for this book, the ideas presented here are entirely ours. We believe, however, that we have remained faithful to the Social and Rehabilitation Services mandate.

Madison, Wisconsin　　　　　　　　Michael Aiken
September 1975　　　　　　　　　Robert Dewar
　　　　　　　　　　　　　　　　　Nancy DiTomaso
　　　　　　　　　　　　　　　　　Jerald Hage
　　　　　　　　　　　　　　　　　Gerald Zeitz

Contents

Coordinating
Human Services

New Strategies for Building

Service Delivery Systems

1

Problem of Coordination

A true story illustrates what it is like to be a multiple-problem client in a delivery system in the United States (California Legislature, Assembly Office of Research, 1969, pp. 1-3):

> Steven A. is a severely mentally retarded boy, sixteen years old, who lives with his father in Santa Cruz, California. Steven and his father moved to this area in 1966, when Mr. and Mrs. A. got a divorce. Mrs. A. lives in another part of the state with Steven's brother and sister.
>
> Steven was referred to the Santa Cruz County Diagnostic and Counseling Center in October 1967 and went through the clinic in November 1967. At that time the clinic staff recommended that Steven be placed in the farm training program conducted by the county superintendent of schools. On November 27, 1967, Steven was enrolled at the farm training school. At first, Steven was extremely difficult to handle; however, he made a slow but steady progress and in a matter of months had adjusted well to the program and was developing good social and work attitudes.
>
> On January 28, 1969, the case of Steven came up at the farm staff meeting. Eve Pecchenino, Steve's teacher,

reported that Steve was very upset because his father planned to take him from the farm training school early in February and to place him in a state institution at Porterville, California. Len Thigpin, farm coordinator, called Steve's father to inquire about his plans, but the father was vague and evasive. There was general agreement at this time that institutionalization would be detrimental to Steve and should be avoided if at all possible.

On January 31, 1969, Thigpin learned that a court hearing would be held on February 3, 1969, to determine whether Steven should be placed at still another institution, Agnews State Hospital. When Thigpin and Bill Carmichael, a teacher at the farm, visited Mr. A. to ask him why he had requested such a hearing, Mr. A. replied that he could no longer provide the proper care and supervision that Steven required. He agreed, however, to allow Steven to stay in the community if an alternative arrangement could be made.

John Tuck, social welfare representative for the Diagnostic and Counseling Center, found a foster home that could accept Steve. This was a home provided by the State Department of Mental Hygiene. Unfortunately, however, Mr. A. could not afford the amount (over two hundred dollars a month) required to keep Steven in a mental hygiene home. Furthermore, since mental hygiene homes are not licensed by the Bureau of Social Welfare Community Services, the cost could not be paid by that agency. A call to the Bureau of Social Welfare Community Services determined that a mental hygiene home cannot be double licensed or licensed as a family-care home, and there were no vacancies in any of the licensed homes in the Santa Cruz area or the nearby area of Watsonville. Finally, a teacher at the farm training school agreed to take Steven into her home until a placement could be made. Mr. A. was happy with this arrangement; he said that he did not want the boy out of the community but did not feel that he had any choice because of the responsibility.

Driving back from the court hearing (where the case was temporarily set aside), Steven turned to Thigpin and said, "They told me you were a good guy and they sure were right." Len asked him what he meant and Steven answered simply, "You came and got me."

By February 5, 1969, in the course of his efforts to find available funds for Steven's care and an agency that would accept responsibility for the boy, Tuck had—without results—contacted the following agencies: Porterville Outpatient Clinic, Porterville State Hospital, Agnews State Hospital, the Department of Mental Hygiene, the Bureau of Social Welfare Community Services (Santa Cruz and Salinas offices), the Office of Education and the Welfare Department of Santa Cruz County, the Welfare Department and the Probation Office and the Office of Education of San Benito County, and the Vocational Rehabilitation Services. After all of these contacts, he was still unable to determine what, if any, funds were available for Steven's care in the community.

To place Steven in an institution would cost the state more than $4000 a year. To keep Steven in a good program in a mental hygiene home in the community would cost the state approximately $2500 a year. But, more important, Steven had made excellent progress at the farm school. Because the channels of communication were muddy and because no one was willing to accept responsibility for the funding of Steven's care, this boy remained in limbo. The tragedy is not that these agencies are not doing their job; the tragedy is that the agencies do not seem to be aware of one another and certainly are not aware of each other's job.

These gaps in service due to lack of coordination, inflexibility of categorically defined programs, and absence of services for one reason or another (but especially due to unavailability of needed funding) translate into tragedies for those with chronic and multiple-service needs. These combined concerns have led in recent years to a new field of interest for those in the social services. This new field is the planning and implementation of integrated and coordinated service delivery systems; that is, organizational systems or sets of organizations that obtain resources from their environments, transform these resources into programs and services, and deliver them to clients.

Faced with a bewildering array of categorical, "added-on" programs and a variety of specialized, incomplete, and sometimes competing programs, professionals debate about the best means to bring coherence and order to the social-service maze. Increasingly, one hears concepts like "service integration" (Buttrick, 1973), "social-service delivery systems" (Kronick, Perlmutter, and Gummer, 1973; Boettcher, 1974), and "social-service system" (F. J. Kahn, 1972). Neighborhood-center concepts have been proposed (March, 1968; O'Donnell and Sullivan, 1969); existing multiservice arrangements have been examined (O'Donnell and Reid, 1972); and some thoughtful questions have been posed about the desirability of such arrangements (N. Gilbert, 1972).

Many barriers and problems confront practitioners who want to assure that the right service is delivered to the right client in the right sequence. The barriers most often mentioned are fragmentation of services (March, 1968; N. Gilbert, 1972), inaccessibility of services (N. Gilbert, 1972), lack of accountability of service delivery agencies (March, 1968; N. Gilbert, 1972; F. J. Kahn, 1972), discontinuities in services (N. Gilbert, 1972), dispersal of services (March, 1968), wastefulness of resources, ineffectiveness of services, short-term commitments. These are symptoms of fundamental barriers, such as organizational autonomy, professional ideologies, conflicts among various client interest groups, and, perhaps most critical, conflicts over who is to control resources. Together these barriers account for the fragmentation of services and the lack of funding. Nowhere are such problems and dilemmas more evident than in the area of mental retardation.

These fundamental barriers to cooperation often are erected by the very groups that should be the ones most involved in the coordination of services. Professional ideologies, for instance, often keep professionals in one field from wanting to cooperate with professionals in another field. Competing client interest groups may cancel out each other's efforts rather than present a united front in the community. And service organizations often put their own survival and prestige ahead of the needs of the clients. Studies show that the acceptance of clients in social service organizations depends on social, cultural, and historical factors, and not just on the needs of the clients (Freidson, 1966; Cumming, 1968; Fried, 1969). Agencies refer clients to places that profit the agency, rather than to places good for clients (Greenly and Kirk, 1973). And agencies like to have the "right" clients—frequently those most responsive to services or those likely to win public sympathy—rather than those with the most pressing problems.

These problems and barriers are especially evident in the area of mental retardation, where the need for coordination and integration of services is great. The mentally retarded are likely to need services in a wide variety of areas for their whole lives. And, further, the historical reluctance to deal openly with mental retardation still to some extent decreases awareness of those services that are available. Thus mental retardation is an especially good area for studying the general problem of coordination and integration of social services.

But these problems are by no means absent in other fields. The health-care system exhibits many of the same inefficiencies that the services for the retarded exhibit, especially if the patient is afflicted with a disabling or chronic disease. Rising costs, questionable quality of care, inequity of access, and other problems of health-care delivery in the United States stem from diverse causes. Professional autonomy is strong, and the services of individual practitioners are not well coordinated with those of hospitals and clinics (Duff and Hollingshead, 1968). Hospitals and individual practitioners are not always distributed geographically according to need (Somers and Somers, 1961; Lynch, 1972). The pressures from professional and other private interest groups often give rise to policies that may be good for professionals, hospitals, or some specific group, but not for the community health system (Alford, 1974). Lack of coordination is frequently the result, with particularly bad effects on the multiproblem patient or client, who has increased need for referrals and cooperative treatments.

Similar problems afflict the physically disabled, who often do not know how to take advantage of available funds to purchase services and who find that agencies are reluctant to treat them because of the stigma associated with their disability (Safilios-Rothschild, 1970). Agencies for the blind try to get clients, usually the young, who will win the most sympathy and thus increase their chances for finding support (R. A. Scott, 1969). We are not arguing that all fields are in an equal state of disarray. State bureaus of vocational rehabilitation have noticeably improved the coordination of services for the disabled, and, in health, prepaid group practice schemes such as the

Kaiser system have built in patient referral systems that cut the provision of useless services (Greenberg and Rodberg, 1971). Nevertheless, in these and many other fields a number of problems remain, and only rarely are service delivery systems designed so that each client gets the needed service in the proper sequence and at the proper time.

From our perspective, the overriding requirement for adequate service delivery is coordination, an idea that is overworked, underachieved, and seldom defined. A discussion of service delivery systems can be fruitful only if we first have a clear and unambiguous understanding of the meaning of coordination; one way to arrive at such an understanding is to examine some uses of this concept by others. Indeed, one of our intents is to add to the literature on coordination by suggesting what this word means.

The first aspect of coordination logically is whether all the necessary resources and services are in fact present in the system and available to clients. We call this *comprehensiveness.* While seemingly a basic concept, comprehensiveness is often omitted from discussions of coordination, implying that coordination should be restricted to only those programs and services currently in the system. For this reason critics such as Terryberry (1968) argue that a concept like coordination is inherently conservative and applicable only to stable, unchanging systems. However, we argue that the first concern of attempts at coordination must be whether the system has all the resources and programs necessary to service clients. As technology creates new programs or identifies new client problems, these should be included in considerations of comprehensiveness. If sufficient resources are not present, then efforts must first focus on what can be done to generate additional resources. We cannot speak of coordination of services for a target population such as the mentally retarded if, let us say, only three of ten necessary programs are present. One may speak of coordination among those existing and incomplete elements, but such coordination would be in tension since seven additional program elements considered necessary for the target population are missing.

However, the mere presence of all functionally necessary elements in a system does not of itself imply coordination of those elements. Thus, we also include *compatibility* in our definition of coordination. By compatibility we mean proper linking and sequencing of elements. This concern with sequencing and proper linkages is frequently included in discussions of coordination.

March and Simon (1958), for instance, define coordination as the problem of arranging the signaling system for interdependent conditional activities, and they discuss two methods of coordination as part of their definition: coordination by plan and coordination by feedback, the primary difference being the degree to which activities are standardized. A key aspect of their discussion of coordination concerns the degree of division of labor and specialization of programming, part of our concern with compatibility. Although March and Simon refer primarily to intraorganizational processes, their discussion can be applied equally to the interorganizational processes usually involved in social-service delivery. The essential question is how many program elements can be combined into some workable set of interrelationships so that goals can be mutually achieved; and a central factor determining the nature of those linkages is the degree to which the activity is standardized. The more standardized, the greater the degree to which coordination can be achieved through a plan or set of programmed linkages among program elements; the less standardized the program linkages, the greater the degree to which coordination must be achieved through feedback, which involves the transmission of new information (Hage, 1974, chap. 2). While one can cite a number of exceptions, we argue that the social-service field more often tends to involve this second type of coordination since in most instances client, program, and resource problems are unlikely to be standardized. This is especially the case when the client has multiple problems that require treatment by a large number of different organizations, each of which provides highly specialized services by professionals.

Building on the idea of March and Simon, Thompson (1967) utilizes the concept of coordination as adequate linkages of organizational parts so that objectives can be achieved. Like March and Simon, he emphasizes the degree of sequencing and linkage of various programs or other elements. He relates coordination to three types of interdependence in organizations: pooled, sequential, and reciprocal. Coordination through standardization, or the use of routines and rules, is most appropriate for an organization with pooled interdependence; coordination through a plan is most appropriate for an organization with sequential interdependence; and coordination by mutual adjustment, in which there is a heavy emphasis on communication, is most appropriate for situations characterized by reciprocal interdependence. Here again, the emphasis seems to be on the degree of compatibility, or adequate interfacing and sequencing of program elements.

We therefore conclude that any definition of coordination must include the concepts of sequencing and linking between program elements, and not just their comprehensiveness. The exact type of linkage depends on the nature and extent of the interdependence among elements, although with multiproblem mental retardation clients feedback of information and mutual adjustment are crucial mechanisms.

Finally, we suggest that the definition of coordination must include not only comprehensiveness (all parts existing) and compatibility (existing parts appropriately sequenced and linked) but also *cooperation*—the quality of the relationships between the human actors in the delivery system. Cooperation includes both a behavior component (common effort, joint operation) and an attitudinal component (willingness to work together, absence of selfishness). Clearly, both are important. Organizational theorists of the human relations school stress the importance of favorable attitudes in achieving coordinated action. Likert (1967), for instance, sees cooperation, in the sense of "favorable attitudes and confidence and trust," as a necessary condition of coordination within the organization, and this would seem to apply even more to relationships between organizations. Others have suggested that agreement about organization "domains"—what each organization should be doing—facilitates coordination (Levine and White, 1961). We therefore define cooperation as the quality of relationships between the human actors in a delivery system so that there is mutual understanding, minimum shared goals and values, and an ability to work together on a common task.

We do not necessarily see conflict as the opposite of coordination. Although excessive conflict may easily prevent coordinated action, minimal conflict may prove to be consistent with coordinated action and may even prove to be positively helpful (Coser, 1956). Cooperation carried on despite some conflict has been referred to as "antagonistic cooperation" (Guetzkow, 1966) and might be helpful, for instance, in bringing to light all the various dimensions of clients' needs. Thus, a fire inspector may initially oppose putting retarded clients in small residential homes because the buildings do not meet institutional safety standards. A counselor, however, may find small homes vital because they provide the atmosphere needed for personal growth. Much conflict may exist, but cooperation in our sense takes place if all can agree that rehabilitation, not just custodial care, is the goal of treatment; if all can have some respect for others' points of view; and, most important, if all are willing to work together and make the compromises necessary to settle differences. The controversy raised might mobilize public opinion and put pressure on the legislature to provide funds for outside fire escapes and other necessary equipment to bring the small homes up to institutional standards.

Given these considerations, we define coordination as the articulation of elements in a social-service delivery system so that comprehensiveness of, compatibility among, and cooperation among elements are maximized. We are suggesting, then, that coordination is a property of a social system (see Mayer, 1970), although the degree of integration and articulation of that system and hence the degree of coordination may vary considerably. By comprehensiveness we mean the extensiveness and fullness of the components that should logically be a part of a delivery system given a statement of its goals. Unless a sufficient number of elements needed to attain some desired state exist, coordination will be impossible to achieve. By compatibility we mean the degree to which components are linked together in some coherent manner; that is, there must be a fit between need and service, and services must be provided to clients in a meaningful and appropriate sequence. By cooperation we mean the degree to which collaboration and integration exist among the elements in a system. In the context of service delivery systems, this refers to collaboration among the congeries of agencies, professions, client groups, and resource controllers so that social services are delivered to clients.

Elements Requiring Coordination

At least four key elements must be coordinated in a fully integrated service delivery system: programs and services, resources, clients, and information (see Table 1). Each of these is an important and essential ingredient in any fully integrated service delivery system, for the coordination of any one of these components does not necessarily imply the coordination of another. The absence of a given element may, however, place serious constraints on the attainment of one of the others. We emphasize these four elements at the outset of our discussion since the various projects for the mentally retarded described in subsequent chapters emphasized different elements, and certainly no project coordinated all four. Any proposal that does not specifically consider all four elements to be coordinated will be unlikely to result in the creation of a fully integrated service delivery system.

Programs and services. The conditions resulting in inadequate coordination of programs and services have been mentioned above and need not be repeated here. For example, in a given community there might be five or six different family agencies involved in the adoption of interracial infants, each with some complementarity in terms of access to donors, access to recipients, or other activities. Each agency chooses to deal with different types of donors and recipients (different religions, amounts of education, locations, and so on). Thus the agencies are not direct competitors and may benefit from program coordination. Yet because of differing traditions, jealousies, or other reasons, program coordination does not

Table 1

Elements Requiring Coordination

| System Element | Aspect of Coordination | | |
	Comprehensiveness	Compatibility	Cooperation
Programs	all needed services; a continuum of care	all needed sequences; all needed joint programs	professionals work together and with other parties
Resources	all needed funds and autonomy	correct allocation on basis of client need and case load	resource controllers work together and with other parties
Clients	all eligible clients are treated and in all areas in which they have needs	services are received in correct sequence consistent with individual needs	client representatives work together and with other parties
Information	central record keeping (clients), directory of services (programs), knowledge about available resources, and continuous feedback relative to the operation of the system at all three levels		

develop. Cooperation implies that the professionals operating the programs have consistent operating philosophies and good working relationships with professionals in related programs. Cooperation at the program level is often aided by informal relationships among professionals, such as membership in the same professional associations or simply meeting for lunch or cocktails.

Comprehensiveness of the service implies a full array of programs related to this service; that is, there is a continuum of care in the sense that the service delivery system contains all the programs and services necessary for a given type of client (see March, 1968). Compatibility of these services means that they are linked together so that transition from one stage of a service modality to another is smooth and uninterrupted; further, it implies that the sequencing of services within this modality is coherent; finally, it implies that overlap and duplication are minimized.

Resources. Coordination of resources often means the integration of funding, although other resources, such as the sharing of a physical plant, are involved in a fully integrated service delivery system.

Comprehensiveness of resources means that adequate resources exist to provide the information, programs and services, and client management in a fully integrated service delivery system. The lack of funds is probably the single biggest deficiency of most delivery systems. Especially where it is necessary to develop a whole new continuum of care for multiple-handicap clients such as the deaf and blind, the lack of resources prevents any meaningful discussion of coordination. Sometimes there is a complete array of programs but they are financed at such low levels that only a few clients are able to take advantage of them. Although we emphasize funding, one other important resource is power. It is hard to separate the two because one often measures a powerful delivery system by its ability to get adequate funds and vice versa. In the case studies, this double theme of power and money occurs again and again.

Compatibility of resources means that resources are provided and administered so that they flow to appropriate targets in such a way that duplication, waste, and needless overlap are reduced or avoided. Frequently, the programs with the most clients do not get the most funds. Usually middle-class and white client groups, which are less numerous, receive a greater proportion of the funds; and working-class and black client groups, which are more numerous, receive a lesser proportion. Also, some organizations or agencies in a delivery system can gain power and as a consequence receive a disproportionate share.

Cooperation implies a consistent set of values controlling the use of resources. Concretely, such coordination involves the integration of resource controllers—that is, various government agencies and private agencies that control funding and thus have power over organizations in the service delivery system. Each of these resource controllers has different values and therefore different priorities. Enough cooperation among resource controllers must be achieved so that all values are represented and they do not cancel out each other's efforts. One can conceive of a somewhat coordinated delivery system that did not incorporate all funding sources at the outset, preferring to work gradually toward expansion of its scope. However, such a system would suffer from inadequate programming and might in the end not have the power to expand.

Client access. Any service delivery system must make sure that a client receives the proper services in the proper sequence. Others have referred to this idea as "case management," "case integration," "case accountability," and "case monitoring" (see F. J. Kahn, 1972).

Comprehensiveness in this context refers to the degree to which all potential clients are identified and treated. In some delivery systems—for example, medical care—there is a reasonable range of services and fairly adequate levels of funding, but not all clients are serviced. Welfare programs often are underutilized because the clients have not been made aware of their benefits. And in some instances a client is partially treated but does not receive all the services he needs. To remedy these problems, there is need for a case coordinator who periodically monitors the situation of the clients. The frequency of monitoring depends to a great extent on the degree of dependence of the client; mentally retarded clients in general are particularly dependent.

Compatibility here concerns the sequencing of services: Is the system organized in such a manner that clients get services when they need them? There is some correct order of treatment, presumably different for different clients, at different ages, and with different combinations of handicaps or needs. However, since there is usually not much monitoring, the client moves from agency to agency somewhat randomly and not in a proper sequence—if he moves at all. Typically clients with multiple problems receive only part of the services they need.

Finally, cooperation refers to the ability of different client, professional, and other interest groups to reach workable compromises that do not subvert the interests of any one group. Different client groups have different interests; in particular there is a fundamental split between working- and middle-class clients and their needs, desires, and feelings. Moreover, professionals and clients have different and sometimes conflicting interests or values; professionals want autonomy, and clients want a say in how services are given as well as individual treatment. Finally, taxpayers from all classes often have different interests from those who need or give services.

Accountability, or more often the lack of it, has been identified as a central problem in service delivery. A basic aspect of accountability is whether the system is responsive to the needs of clients (N. Gilbert, 1972). The accountability problem is in part addressed through case monitoring and coordination. One possibility here is that case managers play the role of ombudsmen, who intervene in the system on the part of their clients. While the role of case coordinators can be defined in a variety of ways, the problem of accountability is addressed in part, though not completely, through case coordination and management.

Information. Coordination of information has both an internal and an external aspect. The external aspect concerns the degree to which information about service opportunities is available to those who are not yet in the system but who seek to make use of it. Information should be made available at some specific site, such as an advice and referral center (March, 1968) or a neighborhood information center (F. J. Kahn, 1972). In a fully integrated service delivery system, the availability of information would be comprehensive in the sense that service inventories (of service-rendering agencies, their programs and services, and the availability of the services) would exist (see Kronick, Perlmutter, and Gummer, 1973). Compatibility in this context implies the existence of a central or fixed point of referral. Cooperation implies that this information is available and accessible to everyone.

The second aspect of the coordination of information is an internal one. It involves the operation of service delivery systems themselves and questions of evaluation and feedback (F. J. Kahn, 1972): Are programs accomplishing the goals they were designed to achieve? Are adequate services available to all clients? Do case managers report that their clients are receiving all the services they need, when they need them, and in the correct sequence? Are there adequate feedback mechanisms and consequent authority to take corrective actions when system deficiencies are identified? In order to respond to questions like these it is necessary to have adequate mechanisms and consequent authority to take corrective action when system deficiencies are identified. Given that services for retarded clients are interdependent, a high degree of information feedback rather than central planning for each client is likely to be most effective.

Coordination of such information would be comprehensive if there were information channels from all parts of the service delivery system so that an assessment of system effectiveness could be made. It would be compatible to the extent that it included assessments of interdependence among various program and service components and their impact on each other. It would be cooperative to the extent that communication channels were open, assuring the free flow of information to and from the control center and various system parts.

Relationships among elements. One way to conceive of these elements is to see them arrayed on a vertical axis by level:

institutional, organizational, and individual. We argue that resources are best coordinated at the institutional level, programs
at the organizational level, clients at the individual case-worker
level, and information at all three levels.

There are different problems of coordination for each
level. At the institutional level, the problem is primarily one of
gaining sufficient resources from the environment of the service
delivery system: for example, funding from federal, state, and
local governments as well as private sources. At the organizational level, programs and service components are invariably
conceived, developed, and delivered by service delivery organizations, whether a county welfare department, a private rehabilitation organization like Goodwill Industries, or a local mental
health center. Whether these programs and services are concentrated in a single superagency or scattered across a host of
autonomous agencies that may offer competing and overlapping
programs, the central problem is linking these diverse program
elements into a coherent "system" of service delivery. The
recipient, or consumer, of the service delivery system is best
coordinated at the level of the individual case worker. The critical problem here is to ensure that the client has the services
needed in the proper sequence and at the proper time. Finally,
information needs to be coordinated at all levels of the service
delivery system—that is, information about obtaining resources
from the environment, transforming these resources into programs and services, and delivering them effectively to clients.

Coordination at one level, therefore, does not imply coordination at another. One could conceive of a delivery system
built around a commitment to coordination at the client level—
a system with an extensive system of case management and case
monitoring. Even if this system delivered all the services a client
needed, in the sequence he needed them, and when he needed
them, it would not necessarily be a coordinated system of service delivery organizations or one which adequately coordinated
resources. To take the other extreme, in a system with optimal
planning, in which such a high degree of coordination was
achieved among service delivery organizations that all services
logically needed by a client population were available, it would
not necessarily follow that all clients were obtaining the services

they needed when they needed them and in the appropriate sequence. Similar arguments could be made about a service delivery system that had optimized the coordination of resources and information.

In any service delivery system that is accessible, responsible and accountable, continuous, effective, efficient, permanent, and planned, specific attention has to be given to the coordination of each of these elements since, we argue, the presence of one does not necessarily imply the presence of others. One of the current problems with some proposals for integrated service delivery systems is that they tend to focus on the coordination of one or two of these elements, but not all. As will become clear from the case studies described in subsequent chapters, none of the five projects we investigated included all four elements. No project focused on more than two of these elements. Because of these limited conceptualizations (the projects were obviously constrained by the experiences of the host organizations), each of these projects omitted essential components, which often resulted in major problems for coordinated service delivery for the mentally retarded.

We have not prejudged at this point how coordination as described here can be best brought about. For example, there have been discussions of the degree to which service delivery systems should have centralized control mechanisms, and a continuum running from unitary and centralized to federated and coalitional has been suggested (see Warren, 1967; N. Gilbert, 1972; Litwak, 1964). Not inconceivably, although improbably, each way of organizing service systems could maximize some of these coordination elements while minimizing others. Discussion of such issues, however, is deferred until Chapter Seven, after we have had a chance to examine in detail each of the five attempts to bring about coordination for the mentally retarded.

Institutional Barriers

A number of threads woven into the fabric of American society increase the difficulty of developing a fully coordinated social-service delivery system as we have defined it. Essentially, as the five case studies described in Chapters Two through Six indicate, four major barriers adversely affect coordination. First of all, organizations tend to maximize their own autonomy. Second, professionals become ideologically committed to their treatments as well as their own needs for autonomy. Third, client representatives are concerned about professional control and have conflicting interests about priorities. Finally, resource controllers are divided and uninterested in the problems of the difficult client. Underlying these four factors is a geopolitical one—the separation of metropolitan urban communities into separate political jurisdictions, with a consequent proliferation of organizations, interest groups, and resource controllers.

Even when there is relatively widespread professional recognition of the need to develop new programs and services— for the mentally retarded, for example—and to create a coordinated delivery system, these barriers effectively prevent or curtail the development of such services. Moreover, the creation of an interest group does not necessarily lead to that group's success in achieving its objectives, even when the interest group is composed of middle-class citizens who are highly motivated to do something for their children, as are the parents of most mental retardates. Such groups simply do not have a large enough power base to create the necessary change and to overcome the barriers to coordination. The persistent theme that runs through all five projects is the problem of power—the major conflicts engendered in power struggles and the reasons why there has not been enough power to accomplish the task.

Organizational autonomy. A central tenet of the organizational literature is that leaders of organizations attempt to maximize the autonomy of the organizations which they lead (Thompson, 1967); to decide for themselves how they will spend their money, what programs and services they will provide, and what kinds of clients they will handle. Desires for autonomy often make organizational elites reluctant to enter into interdependent service delivery systems. Although organizations are willing to develop cooperative relationships—to transfer clients (Levine and White, 1961) and even to enter into joint programming (Aiken and Hage, 1968)—they are reluctant to join together in the same delivery system. In short, they are willing to accept symbiotic relationships but not inherently conflictful ones. And because these competing organizations are not brought into the same system, services often are duplicated and funding for individual programs is inadequate.

Given the reluctance of organizations to work with their competitors and to accept some restrictions on their decision making, any proposed service-delivery system must consider a set of inducements. This is largely a matter of making the benefits that accrue from cooperation exceed the costs incurred. Sometimes a benefit-cost ratio favorable to cooperation occurs naturally, and sometimes it can be induced through public policy. The conditions under which either of these alternatives occurs and under which an organization is willing to surrender some of its autonomy are discussed in Chapter Eight.

This problem of organizational autonomy is particularly acute in the United States, where health and welfare services are highly decentralized. In this sense, the problem of the coordinated delivery system is a peculiarly American problem.

Professional ideologies. Different professions develop different perspectives about the main problems affecting the multiple-problem client. Not unexpectedly, each profession generally perceives its own area of expertise as the critical one. Thus, doctors view physical problems as most important; psychologists are sure that the major difficulties are personality or learning ones; social workers have still different views. One of the problems of coordination is that these professions usually must work together if there is to be any successful coordination. For example, if a sheltered workshop is using behavior-modification methods but the client also is in a mental hospital that is not using such methods, then the effectiveness of these methods may be undermined.

In addition to the forces that divide professionals, professional ideologies often conflict with the expectations of clients. Parents, for example, often feel that professionals are not doing enough or are doing the wrong things; professionals in turn look upon the parents as naive and emotional. Admittedly, parents of mental retardates are a difficult interest group to deal with because of the emotional and financial strain caused by their children's disabilities. But we suspect that the professional-client representative controversy is a common barrier in many service delivery systems. One example was the long and bitter controversy between black parents and teachers in New York City when Mayor John Lindsay experimented with community control.

Again, any coordinated delivery system must give careful attention to the problem of professional ideologies and professional norms of autonomy. Inducements must be provided in order to win active cooperation. Imposing some system on professionals can lead to passive resistance that does not help the client at all. Worse yet, extreme levels of conflict can militate against any effective treatment. The challenge is to find a way of obtaining the cooperation of professionals who have conflicting interests with the other parties in a service delivery system.

Clients' interests. Although clients themselves are seldom organized, organizations such as parents associations often act on their behalf. In fact, in the area of mental retardation, parents associations were largely responsible for calling community attention to this untreated problem. In their understandable enthusiasm for getting things done for their children, however, parents may seek to control what is being done. One of our case studies, that of Bridgeport, illustrates this inherent dilemma about concerned parents. Their energies are necessary; and yet, if they dominate the control of the service delivery system, the professionals involved may cease to cooperate. The reverse is equally a problem.

Moreover, different client groups have different interests and resources. The interests and resources of middle-class parents are not the same as those of working-class parents. The needs of blacks are not the same as those of whites. These conflicting interests frequently cause a cancelation of effort rather than a channeling of energy.

Any service delivery system, again given the special context of American society, must confront the conflicting interests of various client groups and their different priorities and resources. To exclude one or another group does not solve the problem but results only in long-term defeat, especially when it comes to gaining a greater share of resources.

Resource controllers' values. Different resource control-lers at different levels of government—federal, state, county, and city—and in the private sector naturally have different values and therefore conflicts of interest. The federal govern-ment may give seed money to start projects but then argues that the state should continue the project on a permanent basis. Thus, the federal government becomes concerned with innova-tive proposals but not with long-term responsibilities. The states in turn do not want to commit all their scarce resources to inno-vations generated by the federal government. The consequence is that most demonstration projects die because of the inherent conflict of interests between these two levels of government. Private and public resource controllers frequently have different priorities or values as well. Again, the combination of these interests, even though they generate some conflict, seems neces-sary but difficult to achieve. Traditionally the private fund-raising sector has stayed away from those problems confronted by the public sector, and vice versa. Thus, we have another bar-rier to the creation of coordinated service delivery systems.

The problems involved in getting resource controllers to agree about the use of funds are perhaps best appreciated if we study the geopolitical issue of the many separate political juris-dictions at the local level.

Multiple local governments. Approximately two thirds of the people in the United States live in metropolitan areas. In 1962, there were 18,442 local governmental divisions—munici-palities, towns and townships, counties, special districts, and school districts in the 212 Standard Metropolitan Statistical Areas (SMSA) in the United States, or an average of eighty-seven governments in each SMSA. In the twenty-four with a population of one million or more—four of which are included in our study—there were on the average 301 local governmental divisions (Bollens and Schmandt, 1965). These governments overlap in territory and duplicate each other in function, result-ing in highly complex service delivery in metropolitan areas. Added to this complexity is the host of private service delivery organizations—each with its own limited mandate and special clientele. If the metropolitan area can be conceived as a "nat-ural" urban community, then the service delivery mechanisms which have arisen are most often partial, overlapping, incomplete, and uncoordinated.

But there are other consequences of such structural arrangements. Most American cities with populations over five thousand have a council-manager form of government, as opposed to a mayor-council, commission, or town-meeting form of government (Baker, 1971). Further, many of these cities have nonpartisan elections, meaning that political parties are not officially permitted to participate (Lee, 1960). In addition, at-large elections, as opposed to ward elections, tend to accompany council-manager and nonpartisan elections. These elements—together with direct primaries, referenda, small councils, and the short ballot—are aspects of reform government, which has fundamentally altered the governance of American cities (Hofstadter, 1955; Lee, 1960; Banfield and Wilson, 1965). These reforms contributed significantly to the dismantling of urban political machines. At the same time, they also contributed to the depoliticization of the electoral process; the reduction in voting turnout, especially among lower-status persons; the tendency to avoid issues and to concentrate on personality in political contests; the frustration of protest voting; the lack of a feeling of collective responsibility; and a general favoring of conservative interests (see Adrian, 1952; Baker, 1971; Alford and Lee, 1968; Banfield and Wilson, 1965).

Still another aspect of the governmental fragmentation of metropolitan communities has been a consequence of the flight of the middle classes to the suburbs and the expansion of suburban populations in contrast to the central city of metropolitan areas (Schnore, 1965). One result of such population shifts has been the fiscal crisis of central cities as businesses also move into the suburban fringe of the great metropolitan centers. At the risk of some oversimplification, this has resulted in inner cities having a preponderance of black and minority group citizens, the poor or near-poor, and economically induced ills. The problems for creating rational, coordinated service delivery systems not only in education but in public welfare and other areas are virtually insurmountable under these balkanized, depoliticized, and disparate arrangements.

The federal government does not have sufficient power and authority to attack such problems directly, although one could imagine many ways in which the federal government could encourage coordination of service delivery efforts. Since cities are chartered by state governments, the states potentially could also play a role in attempting to reduce the fragmentation of service delivery arrangements in some areas such as education. As a matter of fact, discussions aimed at having the state take over the financing of education have been held in four states: New York, New Jersey, Michigan, and California (Netzger, 1974). The goal of such a move would be to reduce some of the disparities and inequities in delivery of educational services that are so characteristic not only of the metropolitan areas in these states but of many other areas as well. As Shonfield (1969, p. 303) suggests, there is an "American principle of preserving individual freedom by dividing up public authority into separate pieces."

Local governments have a great deal of autonomy vis-à-vis state and federal governments in the United States, compared with the centralized and rationalized structures in countries such as England (see Newton, 1969; Sharpe, 1973). This pluralism is evident in the fragmentation of political units in urban communities, in the variety of auspices of organizations and agencies, in the diversity of religious and ethnic affiliations of agencies, in the many different and autonomous cultural and historical traditions which organizations are reluctant to give up, and in the power of particular professional groupings and associations which often maintain an almost feudal dominion over their service areas. Further, because of political realities, federal programs have often bypassed state, regional, and even urban government levels and dealt directly with local groups, organizations, and departments of government. Because of the multiplicity of partially overlapping government jurisdictions (planning boundaries, school districts, sewer districts), fragmentation of governmental and private services has been intensified (Elazar, 1967; Alford, 1972). Given this fragmentation, attempts at coordination of services at less than the total system level are quite difficult and may even make the situation worse.

For instance, fragmented local services often become loosely organized at the national level, as have the Community Chest drives, rehabilitation agencies such as Goodwill and Cerebral Palsy, community hospitals, and most other services. But this increased integration of local services with national-level umbrella organizations can have the important effect of increasing the resistance to coordination attempts between the various service agencies at the local level (Warren, 1972; Seeley, 1967; Sills, 1957).

This brief description of the pluralism and complexity of American local government and the health and welfare system points up some of the institutional barriers to the creation of coordinated service delivery systems. In summary, the division of the metropolitan community into a variety of different political jurisdictions results in a proliferation of autonomous organizations, parents groups, and resource controllers—all of which cause hurdles in the creation of coordinated delivery systems.

Change Strategies

One way to conceive a coordinated service delivery system is as a change process. Some writers (Hage and Aiken, 1970, chap. 3; Zaltman, Duncan, and Hollbek, 1973) view the change process as having several stages; at each of these stages, certain critical problems and decisions emerge.

The first stage, which might be called awareness of the need for the development of a service delivery system, had occurred prior to the establishment of each of the five demonstration experiments. The President's Panel on Mental Retardation, convened in 1962, had served as a catalytic agent for increased awareness on the part of many practitioners in the field. Actually, this commission was the culmination of a long process of increasing agitation by parents groups and awareness by professional groups that treating the mental retardate requires specialized services, the implementation of which often necessitates new programs.

In the second stage, the initiation of the demonstration projects, several critical problems emerged—problems of gaining power, legitimacy, and funding. In other words, how does one obtain the cooperation of other organizations, each desirous of maintaining its autonomy? What approach is used to gain the cooperation of different professionals? What tactics are employed with the various client representatives to ensure their cooperation? The ways in which these projects attempted to answer these questions is an important aspect of our case histories. In Chapter Seven, they form the basis for our discussion of alternative strategies to those employed in these cities.

How does a community create a coordinated service delivery system? At minimum, and at the risk of some oversimplification, two approaches might be employed. The clients or members of the community might be organized into a powerful interest group, which then puts pressure on private agencies and public bodies in order to obtain sufficient resources to establish what is hoped will be a coordinated service delivery system. The other method would be to organize all those elites in the community who could contribute to the successful establishment and implementation of a coordinated system of services. Variants of the elite-mobilization method of community organization were used in two of the demonstration projects—Cleveland and Los Angeles. The details of the procedures utilized in these two cities are given in subsequent chapters. However, the Los Angeles case involves a considerable departure from what is considered the typical method of elite mobilization. Cleveland is the only city among these five in which traditional community-organization strategies were employed; the strategies utilized in Bridgeport, Milwaukee, and San Francisco are still different.

Closely allied to the problem of power is the question of funding. In most of the demonstration projects, the grant from the federal government was the main source of funding. The whole issue of having the federal government provide demonstration grants is a critical problem which we discuss in Chapter Seven. In most cases, the federal government, by giving too much or too little, largely prevented the success of the demonstration project.

Once power and funds have been obtained, the third stage—implementation—begins. At this stage an organizational structure or delivery mechanism is created for implementing change and coordinating what is done. Many of the demonstration projects ran into a number of difficulties as a result of the choice of the structure for service delivery. Some developed a number of internal conflicts, others prevented any hope of coordination, and most had no effective control over other organizations.

One of the significant differences between the various projects was which element each attempted to coordinate. Some concentrated on client coordination, others on program coordination, and still others on resource coordination. All attempted some form of information coordination. None of the projects attempted to coordinate all four components. We feel that the different demonstration projects did not understand what complete coordination involves and therefore did not construct the appropriate structure for accomplishing their goals. Indeed, we hope that this book can lead to increased awareness of the issues involved in coordination.

Of particular interest, and again an important part of any change process, is the transformation of the goals of the change agent. As failures in achieving objectives occurred, the goals of the demonstration projects became displaced. That is, the change agents scaled down their objectives, concentrating on the particular goals that reflected their inherent interests and values.

Independent of the organizational structure for introducing change in some delivery system is the problem of how much activity or implementation occurred. Although not all the projects had as a stated goal the development of a coordinated delivery system, all promised to implement a number of new programs for the mentally retarded that would fill in the existing gaps in service. We therefore analyze, toward the end of each chapter, how effective these projects were in this regard and the reasons for their relative successes and failures.

A major problem in the implementation stage is the resistance generated. As we have already suggested, the sources of resistance are many in any change process as vast as the creation of coordinated delivery systems. The organizations want to maintain their autonomy. Various political jurisdictions are unwilling to cooperate. The clients and the professionals have different and conflicting notions of what needs to be done, and each group wants to maximize its independence and control. Under these circumstances we have an ideal laboratory for studying all the practical problems involved in implementing change because all these issues are involved in the five projects. For various reasons that shall become clear in the analysis, some of the projects illustrate certain problems more than others. But the five case studies combined show clearly how difficult large-scale change is, at least given the strategies that were employed and the funding involved.

In some of the projects, the San Francisco and Bridgeport projects in particular, conflicts became manifest and ultimately destroyed attempts at goal attainment. We have therefore paid some attention to how these conflicts developed, what issues and interests were involved, and how the destructive aspects of these conflicts might be eliminated. However, even where these conflicts got out of hand, they still had the important function of making clear the latent interests in the retardation community and therefore should serve as lessons for those who are interested in designing such projects in the future.

At the final stage of the change process, routinization, the changes become institutionalized. In this last stage, the resource controllers become critical. Without their support, even the best of programs or of service delivery systems is doomed to fall apart. To provide this support, local governments must convince taxpayers that taxes should be increased. These are formidable change problems indeed. Thus, the issue of what happened to the demonstration projects when their period of federal support had ended is critical.

2

Professional Association: San Francisco

The Coordinating Council on Mental Retardation (CCMR), a voluntary association of professionals from various public and private agencies, was the recipient of the five-year demonstration grant in San Francisco. The San Francisco project shared many of the general urban problems faced by the other projects —lack of services, lack of a fixed point of referral, organizational autonomy, multiple governmental jurisdictions, and a declining tax base. However, because the intervention point for the CCMR was a single organization, it encountered special obstacles in obtaining its primary goal of coordination of services to the mentally retarded. The original goal of the CCMR project was to provide a limited area with extensive and comprehensive services for the mentally retarded, to demonstrate that comprehensive service delivery systems are less expensive in the long run than piecemeal, fragmented programs.

During the 1960s, there were two important changes in the population of San Francisco. First, the city lost population to the surrounding Bay Area. Between 1960 and 1970, the population of San Francisco decreased from 740,316 to 715,674, while the population of the entire Bay Area increased from 2,648,762 to 3,109,519. The second major change was a shift in the composition of the population toward a higher proportion of blacks, Mexican-Americans, Chinese, Filipinos, Japanese, and of those from other racial or ethnic groups. The increase in the black population in San Francisco was consistent with changes in California as a whole; the black population increased 60 percent during this decade.

In the early 1960s San Francisco, like most other cities in the country, provided few services exclusively for the mentally retarded. Although most public service agencies included the less severely retarded among clients receiving welfare, vocational rehabilitation, corrections, or other services, the major services available to mentally retarded children in San Francisco beyond these general welfare services were at Sonoma State Hospital in Eldridge, California. In San Francisco, state money could not be used to provide services to a mentally retarded client unless he had first been hospitalized and then released. Because of the lack of services and this funding procedure, Sonoma had a large waiting list of retarded to be institutionalized.

Initially, all screening and recommendation to Sonoma State Hospital was done by the local Community Mental Health Service Child Guidance Clinic. In 1961, however, the newly appointed program chief decided that such screening was an inappropriate function for Community Mental Health and thus arranged for the state hospital to do its own screening. An announcement to this effect was sent to all agencies serving the retarded in San Francisco. Moving this service from the local community to the less accessible hospital (two hours by car) created a strong reaction among the professionals working with the retarded, particularly in the largest parents group, Aid to Retarded Children. Consequently, a meeting was arranged for the executive directors of all agencies in the city who served the retarded to discuss the issue of screening for Sonoma State Hospital. Although few executive directors attended, most sent a representative. The meeting brought to the surface the many mutual problems faced by agencies serving mentally retarded clients. The Sonoma issue was never discussed, but the group decided to continue to meet regularly in order to pursue in depth the problems of service delivery to this target population. In June 1963, this group was incorporated as the CCMR. Members of the association discussed at this time the need to include nonprofessionals among the membership, including relatives of the retarded, businessmen, and other interested citizens. After some disagreement, the decision was eventually made to exclude lay membership. This decision was to continue to be a major source of controversy for the association and at times to hamper its effectiveness.

Most early members of the CCMR whom we interviewed agreed, however, that as a professional association the CCMR represented at its outset most of the agencies in the city providing services for the mentally retarded. However, as stated in one of the interim reports of the council, most of these services (which were primarily generic) were provided by only six or seven agencies (D. Miller, 1967). Several public (especially state) agencies provided the greatest volume of services. These included the State Department of Mental Hygiene, the State Department of Social Welfare, the San Francisco Unified School District, the San Francisco Department of Public Welfare, and the San Francisco Department of Public Health (including the Community Mental Health Mental Retardation Program and the Golden Gate Regional Center). In addition, two private agencies were important actors in the mental retardation field in San Francisco. These were Aid to Retarded Children and the Recreation Center for the Handicapped.

The State Department of Mental Hygiene is responsible for a number of local programs involving routine health maintenance, day services, and licensing, as well as being in charge of the Langley Porter Neuropsychiatric Institute and Sonoma State Hospital. The State Department of Social Welfare was formerly responsible for community placement from Sonoma and currently continues a range of programs involving case finding and identification, case management, out-of-home care, day homes, social functions, a manpower-development service, and licensing for caretaker homes. The San Francisco Unified School District provides a range of educational services, including the Development Centers for Handicapped Minors, special education for children and adults, parents' education, and day care, in addition to diagnostic services, case finding and identification, case evaluation, and some case management. The San Francisco Department of Public Welfare provides the standard welfare services. The San Francisco Department of Public Health is the umbrella for two major programs for the retarded: the Community Mental Health Mental Retardation Program, which provides public information, case management, and social-functioning services; and the Golden Gate Regional Center, which provides public information, case finding and identification, case evaluation, case management, out-of-home placement, and routine health maintenance.

Aid to Retarded Children (ARC), is the largest parents group in San Francisco and one of the leaders in the field of mental retardation in the San Francisco area. It was primarily responsible for the development of the CCMR project. In addition to various advocacy services, such as informal lobbying, ARC runs an adult training center, a preschool training center, a social-development center, and a vocational evaluation program; it became the administrative agent for the Golden Gate Regional Center when it opened in 1965. The Recreation Center for the Handicapped grew to be an important agency for the mentally retarded during the 1960s. During this period its clientele had shifted from the physically handicapped to primarily the mentally retarded. In addition to recreation services, the center also runs a day-care program, a camping program, and a multitude of day activity services.

These are the major agencies providing services to the mentally retarded in San Francisco, although other agencies also do. Despite the number of agencies, however, the range of services available to the retarded is not complete. Some services are given higher priority than others, and none of the agencies providing services has the capacity to handle all clients in need.

Awareness Stage

New legislation for the retarded in California evolved in some ways accidentally. After a national report on the state of services to the mentally retarded (President's Panel on Mental Retardation, 1962) was issued, California began to take stock of its programs and services for the mentally retarded. However, it was a news story about the poor conditions at Fairview State Hospital in Orange County which led to the appointment of a study commission by Governor Edmund G. Brown. At the same time, a legislative committee was set up for the same purpose under the chairmanship of the leader of the majority caucus of the California assembly, Jerome Waldie. In January 1965, the governor's commission published its report, entitled *The Undeveloped Resource*; two months later, the legislative committee published its report, *A Redefinition of State Responsibility for California's Mentally Retarded*. The governor's commission recommended increasing the capacity of state mental hospitals so as to decrease the waiting lists; the legislative report, in contrast, called for developing community resources so as to minimize the need for state mental hospitals. The legislative recommendations prevailed: in 1965 Assembly Bill 691 created two experimental regional centers, one in San Francisco (the Golden Gate Regional Center) and one in Los Angeles. Each was to serve as a "fixed point of referral" and a "continuum of care," as recommended in the report of the President's Panel. The specific mandate for the regional centers was to serve those on the waiting lists for state hospitals by contracting community services for them, presumably at a lower cost than that of keeping a patient in a state hospital. This bill was to have a tremendous effect on changes in services for the mentally retarded in California. The "conceptual breakthrough" of this shift in service delivery (as one interviewee put it) was the possibility of buying private services with public funds and, in general, of increasing the utilization of local, community services. This legislation was also to have a tremendous effect on the activities of the CCMR in San Francisco.

Among the activities of the CCMR were several professional workshops for ministers, public health nurses, social workers, and others concerning services for the mentally retarded. In one of these workshops the idea for an information and referral service developed. In 1964, a three-year demonstration grant to establish such a service, under the joint sponsorship of the CCMR and the Community Mental Health Service, was obtained from the National Institute of Mental Health. The program was officially run by the Community Mental Health Service, with the CCMR acting as the fiscal agent. In addition, the CCMR obtained a $20,000 grant under the National Mental Health Act from the State Department of Mental Hygiene, hired an executive director, and began organizing a program. Under the first executive director, funds were also obtained from the San Francisco Foundation for the publication of a professional newsletter, the *Coordinator*.

Initiation Stage

Early in 1963, several events occurred which eventually altered the nature of the CCMR. At that time Sargent Shriver, attending a local ARC function, suggested that San Francisco would be an excellent location for demonstrating that blanketing an area with services would be a less expensive approach in the long run than the current hit-or-miss approach to service delivery. His encouragement led to a meeting of the regional director of the Vocational Rehabilitation Administration (VRA) and representatives of ARC, the United Community Fund, Community Mental Health, and the State Department of Mental Hygiene to discuss the possibility of obtaining a grant as part of this plan. The original expectation of obtaining a large amount of funds from several different sources to establish a comprehensive set of community services for the mentally retarded as suggested by Shriver was never to come about, but in 1965 the CCMR applied to the VRA for a small grant, with a limited focus. It should be kept in mind, in later discussions about the confusion of objectives in the project, that the approved grant request was a much scaled-down version of this original plan.

A planning grant was obtained and a researcher hired to do a pilot study before the formal application for the grant was made. The preplanning study examined forty-six cases (out of an estimated retarded population in San Francisco of between 13,000 to 24,000, depending on whether a 1½ or 3 percent criterion is used) provided by CCMR members. In addition, a census of persons known to be mentally retarded was taken at various agencies in San Francisco during October 1964. Four thousand (unduplicated) cases of mental retardation were identified; only 13 percent of these were being served by more than one agency in the city (Miller and Tallenbaum, 1964). The grant went through a number of revisions, deletions, and additions before final approval was obtained in 1965.

The objectives of the demonstration program, as written in the grant proposal, not only lacked specificity but proved to be too optimistic for the resources available. The three general objectives of the grant were as follows: "(1) to initiate action on needed services for the mentally retarded and their families (a) within the existing structure of San Francisco's health, education, and welfare institutions and (b) through new programs which cannot be encompassed within that existing structure; (2) to increase utilization of all services for the mentally retarded through increasing communication, sharing, and understanding of values among professional suppliers of service, among receivers of service, and between the two groups; (3) to provide channels for effective coordination of the development of new and expanded programs to ensure the wisest use of money and manpower for maximum service." These general objectives were subdivided into four short-range and two long-range goals. The short-range goals were to provide services for day care, respite, transportation, and guardianship. The long-range goals were (1) "the coordinated expansion of existing services for the retarded" and (2) "the modification of attitudes and values of both the professional and lay community with respect to use of community services for the retarded."

In terms of our concept of coordination we can see that the objectives of this project mostly involved the themes of comprehensiveness and cooperation and less the theme of compatibility. However, their major focus in practice was on the coordination of clients and less on programs and resources.

The CCMR relied upon a committee structure to effect change. The members of these committees were professionals from various agencies. It was assumed that the professionals could exercise leverage within their particular organizations to bring about the needed changes. There were committees for each of the short-term goals, as well as committees on education, legislation, and so on.

Especially interesting is part of a letter dated June 1965 from the assistant commissioner of the VRA to the president of the CCMR, sent just prior to the approval of the grant: "The emphasis in these projects is service. The concept is based on the continuum of service spoken of in the report of the President's Panel on Mental Retardation. . . . One problem we saw with this project proposal is that it seems to be addressed to all aspects of the mental retardation problem. We would like for it to be highly vocational rehabilitation oriented since the basis for our support is the vocational rehabilitation element. It is hoped that as the project becomes established, it will assist your group to *secure support from other funding sources for parts not related to vocational rehabilitation*" (italics added). This letter clearly indicates that the grant proposal was written with Shriver's original suggestion for a comprehensive push in the area of retardation in mind. It did not explicitly emphasize vocational rehabilitation activities. Only minimal amounts of funding were ever obtained by the CCMR from other sources. The confusion between the VRA goals, the initial CCMR goals, and the goals as enumerated in the grant request grew as the project progressed; in retrospect, it seems clear that this confusion of goals was a major problem with this project.

The four major short-range goals that the CCMR had set for itself and on which it spent most of its time during the five-year grant period were generally directed toward the deinstitutionalization of the more severely retarded. This general goal was articulated in the 1962 report of the President's Panel and was becoming a trend at the state level in California at the time. The mandate of the new regional centers was specifically to become an intervening step between the client and the state hospitals. The goals of the CCMR from the beginning were consistent with this trend. All four of these service categories would be necessary if one were interested in serving in the local community previously institutionalized clients or those requesting institutionalization. None of the four service categories upon which the CCMR focused were directly facilitative for vocational rehabilitation or prevocational training. Although, understandably, the problem of deinstitutionalization loomed large in the minds of the members of CCMR because of the initial incident at Sonoma State Hospital, which led to the formation of the association, the clients to be served by the process of deinstitutionalization would not necessarily be the clients most likely to profit from vocational services. This distinction was the key issue in the confusion over the goals of the CCMR. The services with which CCMR was concerned were not the services considered appropriate by the local vocational rehabilitation agency (nor by the national VRA, which was providing funding for the project), and the clients were not likely to be the same. Therefore, not surprisingly, comments such as the following were made in retrospect by some of the CCMR members: "It was strange that Vocational Rehabilitation funded this project because they have less than anyone to do with mental retardation in the San Francisco area. Almost any other auspices would have been better."

In part the confusion over goals was exacerbated by the high turnover among personnel in the project and members on the board. As new members joined CCMR and old members ceased to participate, the original goals were lost sight of and new ones were defined independent of the original intentions of the funding agency. In addition to the internal confusion among members of the association, there was a general unsettledness in the field of mental retardation across the country. Therefore, the difficulty in defining operational goals for this project was in part a reflection of the general problem outside the San Francisco area.

Conflict over strategy revolved around the distinction between "planning" and "action." Some members thought that the CCMR should limit itself to planning for action—action by someone else; other members wanted to effect planning through action—action by the CCMR itself, to be taken over at a later date by someone else. In essence, this is a manifestation of the problem of lay versus professional membership. The members could not decide whether they wanted the CCMR to be a professional association or an advocacy or interest group. The function of a professional association is usually to keep its members informed of the latest literature, techniques, and information in the field; to report on and sometimes lobby for legislation affecting the profession; and occasionally to arbitrate disputes within the profession. Most normally, it is a forum for information exchange and a means of providing a sense of legitimacy to the profession as a distinct body. An interest or advocacy group does some of these things, but most often it puts pressure where possible to change or initiate activities of agencies in the field of interest. Occasionally, it acts as an entrepreneur for the establishment of new agencies or services. A professional association never competes with its constituents; an interest group by definition usually competes with others in the field or attempts to stimulate competition among existing agencies. Professional associations are ongoing, whereas interest groups are usually organized around specific issues and continue only as long as the issues are salient. When interest groups are long term, they tend to hire professional staff to run day-to-day activities (particularly keeping members informed of possible controversies) and mobilize mass participation only when new issues arise. When any one organization attempts to play both roles, the result is much internal conflict, a great deal of turnover in staff, and unevenness in effectiveness in any one task area. The CCMR fits this description quite well.

Implementation Stage

The San Francisco demonstration project was similar to the other demonstration projects in that there were both advantages and disadvantages to the particular approach and method of programming. The CCMR approach showed considerable strengths as an informational forum and as a force for legitimating the needs for more services for the mentally retarded among professionals in health and social-service agencies. It also engaged in legislative lobbying and program planning. However, its major weakness became apparent in its efforts to get beyond the planning stages to the establishment of services. Although the CCMR perhaps indirectly stimulated the growth of services for the mentally retarded in various agencies, it was not able to seed or to sponsor any new services itself. In the confusion over goals and structure, much discussion was devoted to whether the association should attempt to provide services. Clearly, it did not.

After the CCMR received the grant from the VRA, it directed most of its efforts toward the four short-range goals that it had defined for itself in the grant application. The long-range goals were dealt with, for the most part, through the continuation of its ongoing programs, such as the Information and Referral Service, the case committee (an interagency review committee, established by CCMR, for difficult or multiple-problem cases), and the *Coordinator,* each to be discussed later.

In 1965, the CCMR hoped to accomplish its goals by providing program consultation for the opening of a multiservice center in San Francisco, whose construction would be financed by the state and whose operation would be provided for by the city and county governments. The CCMR worked with the San Francisco County Health Department and the Community Mental Health Service in attempting to accomplish this plan, which was to involve its evolution into a permanent agency of the community within five years. However, in June 1965, the health officer of San Francisco County vetoed construction of the multiservice center in favor of a plan for decentralization of services.* After the multiservice center was vetoed, the CCMR

*Many of the following details on the activities of the CCMR are taken from the final report of the San Francisco project (San Francisco Coordinating Council on Mental Retardation, 1970), supplemented by numerous personal interviews and unpublished reports to the CCMR. The report was prepared by Mary T. Loeb and Lawrence I. Kramer of Kramer, Miller, and Associates. Page numbers from the report are referenced where appropriate.

continued working with the County Health Department and the Community Mental Health Service on the plan for decentralization. At this point, the board-appointed committees previously mentioned began actively seeking other avenues for the furtherance of their goals.

Day care. A day-care committee was set up in the spring of 1964. In December 1965, the day-care committee produced a report on the state of day-care services. In February 1966, discussions were underway concerning the feasibility of opening a day-care center in the Mission area of San Francisco with the joint cooperation of the CCMR, the Mission Neighborhood Center, the Recreation Center for the Handicapped, the Community Mental Health Service, and the Unified School District. The CCMR was to provide some funding for a director; the Recreation Center for the Handicapped was to run the program; the Community Mental Health Service was to provide diagnostic services; the Mission Neighborhood Center was to provide a building; and the Unified School District was to help with identification of cases for the day-care center. The staff of the CCMR began to take steps for setting up the proposed program. At the same time, some members of the board began to feel uncomfortable about the council's providing direct services— that is, being in direct competition with other agencies: "Some unique organization symptoms began to point to a constitutional weakness that was to hamper the council's effectiveness" (p. 29). This "constitutional weakness" was the similarity in the background and training of members of the board and the staff, a similarity that made them "functional peers"; thus, they began to get in each other's way in decision making over the proposed day-care project.

At this time, the board of the CCMR expressed concern that the staff was moving too quickly on the Mission Neighborhood project. The issue of whether movement was quick or not reflected a split between members of this committee—a split which was familiar in general to CCMR. Some members wanted the CCMR, including the day-care committee, to plan but not act. Others wanted the CCMR to provide direct services by use of seed money. The issue of whether the CCMR should provide services was directly confronted when the Mission Neighborhood Center offered to run its own program if CCMR would pay part of the salary for the director of the program. The board of CCMR approved a contract to pay part of the salary for a staff person, but made it clear that it considered the Mission Neighborhood Center primarily responsible for funding. The lack of consensus on this issue within the board led ARC to apply for a grant from the U.S. Public Health Service for a program similar to the proposed day-care center of the council and the Recreation Center for the Handicapped to withdraw its participation on this committee.

After much confusion, ARC decided to operate the social-development center itself, and the Mission Neighborhood Center decided not to continue with plans for the project without funding. In December 1967, the CCMR prepared a report on why the Mission-area program had failed. It also considered replacing the day-activities committee with a committee on habilitation (p. 35). The report attributed the difficulties to staff changes, in both the CCMR and the Mission Neighborhood Center, which prevented continuity and follow-through; the lack of clarity of responsibilities and priorities of all agencies involved; the failure to act at crucial times; and the confusion of the funding caused by the other problems. However, the implications of the day-care project, since it contributed to interagency competition, also need to be considered. By providing funding for a director of the project, the CCMR would have exacerbated underlying competition between two agencies that had representatives in the association. The project was seen by the CCMR as a joint program; but if one considers supplementary services (such as diagnosis, case finding, and perhaps location) as constant, then the agency that was given administrative responsibility, the Recreation Center for the Handicapped, had a definite financial advantage over others in the association who also might have wanted to run the program. In this case, the two major actors seem to be the Recreation Center for the Handicapped and ARC. Both had representatives on the CCMR who were active, and thus either might have objected had the association used part of its funding for support of the other. Both organizations are nonprofit and depend on contributions from lay supporters by way of board contacts and other promotions, and both were interested in providing day-care service. As a consequence, action on a day-care project became blocked through the CCMR, and both ARC and the Recreation Center for the Handicapped set up their own separate programs with outside funding not administered by the CCMR. Had a joint program in which both the Recreation Center and ARC would have participated been the original goal, the program might have been more feasible.

Transportation. The transportation committee, which was also set up in the spring of 1964, was in some ways more successful than the day-care committee. Nevertheless, the efforts of the transportation committee did not produce a transportation service for the mentally retarded, but only a much heralded plan for a transportation service. The service planned by the transportation committee focused on getting moderately and severely retarded individuals to agencies for service, not on teaching the mildly retarded to use public transportation. Furthermore, early in the life of the transportation committee, CCMR members concluded that a program of transportation just for the mentally retarded was not feasible, and therefore they contacted other handicapped groups. In the fall of 1964, the committee sent a questionnaire to all voluntary agencies in San Francisco to assess their interest in the transportation problem. A member of the Red Cross Motor Corps, who eventually became the transportation coordinator for CCMR, was consulted for her advice. This was the only committee for which the CCMR hired a full-time staff member, which should indicate something about the operative priorities of the association. The transportation committee was not defined as being more important than other committees since all the committee goals were impressive. However, if one examines how resources were allocated by the CCMR, transportation evidently was considered one of the more important goals.

Several proposals for a transportation plan were investigated and rejected by the transportation committee before a suitable plan was selected. The earlier plans included the use of public bus transportation, the use of a private transportation firm (which did trial runs for the Recreation Center for the Handicapped and ARC), and the establishment of a new company. The final plan was developed after an extensive simulation of a transportation program in which requests for service were reported but no transportation was provided. After analysis of the simulation, a model for a transportation program was suggested by John P. Carter, a transportation expert with the University of California, Berkeley, School of Business. Carter suggested that any system should be operated in conjunction with an existing company, and bids were eventually solicited from local transportation companies. The final decision was for a five-day-a-week service, using seven vehicles (four radio-dispatched), at a cost of $179,000 per year.

Several local agencies were approached to sponsor the proposed transportation program, but all of them refused because of the magnitude of the program. After much consultation, one of them suggested a joint program in which several agencies would share the responsibility. The San Francisco Hearing Society eventually agreed to administer the program with joint sponsorship by other agencies working with the handicapped. Although the CCMR explored several sources for obtaining funding, including public agencies and private foundations, the program had not been funded at the end of the project.

Respite-care zoning. One short-term goal that the CCMR had set for itself, to provide respite care for families with retarded members, was turned into an attempt to change the zoning ordinances in San Francisco. Respite care is defined as the "availability of care for the retarded individual for twenty-four hours or more when care out of home is required" (p. 21). The trend in California to get mentally retarded patients out of state hospitals was strongly supported by the CCMR, and increasingly more foster-home placements were necessary. However, because of zoning restrictions regarding foster placement, agencies were finding it difficult to locate caretaker homes. The restriction was that in residential areas of the city no mentally retarded adults and no more than two mentally retarded children could be placed in a foster home. The ordinance governing home placement was less restrictive for "normal" children. Two basic issues were involved here. First, there was the difficulty of finding a sufficient number of placement homes. Second, CCMR members felt that the zoning law perpetuated negative attitudes toward the handicapped, particularly the mentally retarded.

The CCMR decided to take a forthright stand against the zoning restriction and to "force a favorable ruling from the City Planning Commission and the Board of Supervisors" (p. 45). Because of this approach, the CCMR was later accused of being naive about the importance of zoning ordinances in local politics and the strength of homeowners associations. One informant said that the CCMR was given a list of names of neighborhood association officials with retarded children but that these were not followed up. The impetus for the action on zoning, according to this same informant, probably came because a zoning change was "slipped through" in Alameda County, although it was later rescinded.

The first direct action that the CCMR took was to call a special meeting of all agencies concerned with licensing and placement in August 1967. At this meeting, the name of the respite-care committee was changed to the ad hoc committee on out-of-home placement, and as a result several members dropped out. By September, the ad hoc committee had drafted a position statement in favor of zoning changes, and it was subsequently passed by the board of directors. The CCMR then solicited similar support from local agencies working with the mentally retarded. By October, legal counsel had been obtained, and the committee formulated specific changes that they would be willing to support. Their goal was to obtain zoning approval for up to six boarders plus supervisory staff. Toward the end of 1967, in several letters from the zoning administrator, the council was warned about the intensity of the opposition to the proposed zoning changes from homeowners associations. Soon thereafter, the council contacted the American Civil Liberties Union (ACLU) about the possibility of a test case to get a court ruling on the issue if necessary.

Little had been accomplished toward change by July

1968, so the CCMR made arrangements for the zoning committee of the City Planning Commission to visit placement homes.
At the same time, local agencies were sending letters of support
for the proposal to the City Planning Commission. In the fall of
1968, the City Planning Commission made recommendations
for change, with a maximum of four placements per home. The
commission met in September to hear the arguments for the
proposal. The CCMR had several heads of agencies testify in
support of the original proposal to allow six placements per
home. Representatives of several homeowners associations testified against the change on the basis of protecting "the integ-
rity of the single-family residential district." A public hearing
was called in November, after which the City Planning Commission recommended the change as supported by the CCMR.
Another public hearing was called in January 1969 before the
Board of Supervisors, but this hearing was dominated by supporters of the homeowners associations and those against the
proposed zoning changes. Among others, a psychiatrist (himself
a vice-president of one of the homeowners associations) testified that "retarded children requiring foster-home placement
were those who were so disruptive that their own parents could
not manage them" (p. 49). In April 1969, the Board of Supervisors ruled that there would be no change. Subsequently, the
CCMR took no further action on zoning except to continue to
seek a test case through the ACLU. A case was found, but a
judge denied the suit. Since then, the California assembly has
passed Assembly Bill 2406, "which defines a 'family,' for zoning purposes, to include up to six handicapped persons placed
by social agencies." As a result, the ACLU asked the judge to
"vacate his decision" (p. 79).

In the opinion of its members, the CCMR could not
effect zoning changes in San Francisco because it did not have a
basis of support in the community. There was also some criticism of ARC for failing to support the CCMR on this issue.
However, this criticism is another way of saying that if there
had been community support, there would not have been community resistance. One need only consider the hostility aroused
by questions of segregation and open housing to understand the

strength of opposition to such questions as zoning (Babcock, 1969). It is not surprising that an organization such as ARC, made up of homeowners and dependent on their support, would not actively support a proposal which could conceivably cut their base from under them. In addition, there are other reasons why parents and homeowners would not be willing to support efforts for increased community placement. One interviewee involved in both the state and national parents associations said, "Many parents pay lip service to the concept of normalization but have deep questions about it on a pragmatic basis. On the one hand, people see foster homes which are understaffed, temporary, and providing bad service, and on the other hand, they see the state hospitals. Parents don't see anything in between, which makes it difficult to reorient money." This statement implies that the uncertainty of the quality of community services (in comparison with the stability of state hospitals) makes it difficult to get even parents of the retarded to support efforts for community placement, such as the attempt of the CCMR to change the zoning ordinance, and therefore it is even more difficult to get the support of homeowners who have no direct interest in the retarded.

Guardianship. On guardianship, another short-term goal, the CCMR did not do much actively as an organization, but it supported the lobbying efforts of ARC for a guardianship bill. Senate Bill 1159 was passed by the California legislature in 1968. The bill allows the director of the State Department of Public Health to be nominated by the family of a retarded person as "guardian, conservator, and advisor." After accepting the nomination, the director designates the regional center to act as his agent. The regional center then officially acts as a "wise parent" to the retarded person. The CCMR role in the passage of this legislation was to keep the professional community informed of the status of the bill. As the final report of the project suggests, the CCMR "left the community and legislative action to the broader-based parent group" (p. 50).

Long-range goals. The long-range goals of the CCMR, which were to bring about the coordinated expansion of services and to modify attitudes and values regarding retardation, were only tangentially approached by the association. The most frequently mentioned benefit of the CCMR was the opportunity it provided for professionals working in mental retardation to get to know one another, to discuss mutual problems in the provision of services, and to learn about other services available in the field. The two projects most often mentioned as facilitating these accomplishments were the case committee (originally called the stymied case committee and later the screening committee) and the publishing of the *Coordinator*. In the minds of some participants, these efforts brought about a degree of community coordination that had not existed before in San Francisco and markedly changed community and professional attitudes toward mental retardation. Members also suggested that two CCMR projects, the Information and Referral Service (currently run by the Community Mental Health Mental Retardation Program) and the *Directory of Services to the Retarded in San Francisco* (published in January 1970), were of assistance in bringing about coordination.

The stymied case committee existed from May 1962 to January 1964; the screening committee, which served the same function, existed from the spring of 1967 until 1970, when its name was changed to the case committee and it was taken over by the Community Mental Health Mental Retardation Program. These committees served as a forum for cooperative case management of difficult (usually multiple-problem) cases. The cases brought before them were voluntary, and thus the committees had to be careful in handling them to assure that other cases would be brought to them in the future. Nevertheless, the fact that clients were going to be discussed caused those involved from various agencies to update their work on the cases. This phenomenon is consistent with the hypothesis that when performances are made public, there is likely to be a tendency toward improved quality.

The *Coordinator* was widely circulated by the CCMR to members and nonmembers, parents, and professionals. Besides articles on the activities of the CCMR, the *Coordinator* included literature reviews, reports on recent research of importance, announcements of upcoming events in fields of interest to members, and reports on programs of local agencies. Many felt that it was an excellent vehicle for keeping those interested in retardation informed. Its frequency of publication had decreased with the end of the demonstration project.

Lanterman Act. The Lanterman Mental Retardation Services Act of 1969 (AB 225) was a continuation and expansion of the 1965 legislation (AB 691), mentioned earlier, which established two regional centers to develop community services for the mentally retarded on an experimental basis. The 1969 Lanterman Act was intended to expand the number of regional centers throughout California so one would be within easy driving distance for anyone needing services. As with the earlier legislation, the underlying goal of the Lanterman Act was to get mentally retarded clients out of large state hospitals and back into the community. Several members of the CCMR had worked on drafts of the Lanterman legislation, as had professionals in the mental retardation field in other parts of the state.

One of the provisions of the bill which was considered a major innovation in the delivery of social services was its development of a program, rather than a departmental, budget at the state level. In other words, money which might have been budgeted for a Department of Health or a Department of Mental Hygiene, for example, was budgeted instead for the retarded as a service category; services could then be bought from any agency that could provide them. The intent of this shift in budgeting procedures was to allow greater coordination of services for clients than had been possible when needed services were located in numerous agencies, each with different requirements for eligibility. The same program concept was developed for service delivery for other types of clients in California after the Lanterman Act was passed for the mentally retarded.

The structure established by the Lanterman Act was also considered innovative. The regional centers established were to become the step between the community and the state hospital. Each regional center was to assume responsibility for diagnosis, counseling, referral, purchasing of service, and permanent guardianship (it became responsible for the clients it accepted for life). The guardianship aspect of the bill was intended to guarantee stability of community services, which had been a major concern of opponents of the original bill. The bill created thirteen area boards to give recommendations to the governor for a state plan. The composition of the area boards was to be 25 percent parents, 25 percent general public and county supervisors, and 50 percent professionals.

One especially controversial aspect of the regional center legislation was that each center was contracted to a local administrative agent, which could be either a public or a private agency. The state employees' union in California had in fact sued the state because of contracts to private agencies. The regional center in San Francisco (Golden Gate Regional Center) was contracted to ARC and was one of those contested in the suit. ARC, along with other private agencies, won and was, therefore, allowed to continue the administration of regional centers. However, a provision of the 1969 legislation would have excluded ARC from participation in the Lanterman Act planning had it not been for the CCMR. The Lanterman Act provision prohibited any employee of a regional center, the State Department of Public Health, the State Department of Mental Hygiene, or the State Department of Social Welfare to be a member of an area board. But, because CCMR was selected to do the San Francisco plan, ARC was allowed some input into the Lanterman Act planning.

The CCMR set up an ad hoc steering committee, engaged several consultants, and hired a research firm to prepare the plan. The CCMR released all staff except the transportation coordinator from other committee duties to enable them to give full effort to the Lanterman Act planning. An official task force was set up in January 1970. In March, six subcommittees were established: Diagnosis, Evaluation, and Treatment; Education and Training; Adult Occupational Activities; Out-of-Home Care; Social Welfare; and Mental Health. The task force was to produce "an inventory of currently available services, an outline of immediate goals, a five-year plan of objectives, and a research plan with a development of innovative models for new and improved methods for serving the mentally retarded. The overall plan would encompass proposals for primary, secondary, and tertiary prevention, as well as consider cooperative projects with other counties where appropriate" (p. 72).

In May 1970, the task force completed a thirty-eight-page report which summarized the work of the subcommittees and outlined several program recommendations for the implementation of the Lanterman Act. The final plan for San Francisco County, to be turned over to Area Board V, was completed in March 1971 under contract to URS Research Company. A former active CCMR member, previously president and chairman of the board, was appointed to the area board and subsequently elected chairman. In June 1971, the area board produced a plan to be presented to the governor.

Analysis of Strategy

Displacement of goals. The language of the various reports of the CCMR demonstration project to the VRA (and later to Social and Rehabilitation Services) had an interesting evolution during the five-year period of the grant. Initially, the association wanted to "initiate action on needed services . . . , to increase utilization of all services . . . , and to provide channels for effective coordination of the development of new and expanded programs." By July 1968, the project reports used such terms as "working with," "developing and demonstrating," "promoting," "pointing out," and "stimulating." Finally, by December 1970, the council defined itself as an organization which provided "idea generation and program stimulation" and served as "a sounding board for specific community problems." The changes represent a continuum from action to planning.

A number of explanations have been given for this shift in intent. Undoubtedly, one explanation, the one given most weight in the final report, is that the composition of both the board and the staff was the same. As a result, there was considerable confusion over who had authority to make decisions; and this confusion, in turn, created a serious morale problem, a general lack of trust between the board and the staff, and high staff turnover. Most of the policy decisions and many administrative decisions (including hiring of personnel) usually assigned to staff were made by the board. Moreover, the board vetoed staff decisions whenever they led to direct action. If a staff member attempted to act independently, he or she was formally or informally asked to resign. The board originally consisted of twelve members but was expanded to twenty-four in 1968 to broaden the professional base. During the entire life of the project, the board clearly dominated all activities (and in many cases board members were the personnel utilized for the implementation of programs), set goals, and supervised staff actions. The links between the board and the officers were also close. Most of the officers also held positions on the board, and often rotated among these positions. In other words, a small group of people dominated these leadership positions during the life of the project.

The small professional staff of the CCMR included (at various times and for varying lengths of time) an executive director, an assistant director (only for a short period of time), a planning grant director (for a short time), a program coordinator, a program assistant (for a short time), an education coordinator, a transportation coordinator, a newsletter staff, a research assistant (for a short time), an administrative assistant (for a short time), and various consultants to evaluate the program, as well as clerical and secretarial help. The twelve professional positions occupied during the five-year project were held by nineteen different people. Seven of the twelve positions were in existence less than two years, and two of the five positions which were in existence for most of the project were filled by different people almost every year. Thus, there was considerable fluidity in both the structure and the personnel of the professional staff.

Another reason for the shift in CCMR goals from action to planning is the conflict among agencies which were members of the CCMR—especially the agencies representing parents and those representing professionals. Since planning and information passage are of approximately equal value to all organizations, the goals were "safe" ones that did not antagonize various organizational interests. Furthermore, the planning engaged in did not call for joint programming by agencies or for penalties for noncompliance. The plans could be safely ignored and thus were not threatening.

Factors affecting implementation of services. The most important factor affecting the implementation of services was the underlying competition among agencies with representatives in the association. Competition for clients, resources, and personnel is always more covert than overt; nevertheless, throughout the history of the CCMR, it occasionally became manifest. To compare the success of the various goals of the CCMR, one needs to consider the differences between tasks that would bring about an organization advantage and tasks that would bring about a system advantage. An organization advantage would bring gains to a single or a small number of organizations, whereas a system advantage would be shared by all organizations in the system of services. (For the classic statement on this problem of individual versus collective utility, see Olson, 1968.)

For example, a day-care center, one of the goals of the CCMR, is an organization advantage; transportation, another goal, is a system advantage. By and large, all agencies, regardless of the age range of their clients and the aspect of retardation with which they are involved, need to be concerned about the provision of transportation, but not about a day-care service. Only some agencies would be directly concerned with day care, depending on the age level of their clients and the aspects of retardation for which they provided services; and, furthermore, those agencies that would be concerned directly with day-care services would in most instances be competing with one another to be the provider of the service. Thus it is more likely that various agencies would cooperate to provide a transportation service, which would be of mutual benefit to all of them, than they would to provide a day-care service, which would benefit only some—particularly the one agency given administrative responsibility for a day-care center. A task which created a system advantage would tend to reduce interagency competition, but a task which created an organization advantage might exacerbate it. If one compares the success of the day-care committee with that of the transportation committee, one can see how the differences in the nature of the task itself could have had an effect on the success of the committee.

An example of how the competition among members of the CCMR may have hampered effectiveness was the extensive discussion and controversy over whether the CCMR should include lay members. As mentioned in the discussion of the CCMR program efforts, the transportation committee—a system advantage—was the only one which utilized lay members with the support of the CCMR board. On other efforts (notably organization advantages like day care), lay people were not included, even though committee members attempted to get approval from the board to include them. Because many of the committee members were also board members, the board itself was split on the issue of lay participation. In the final analysis of the CCMR project, the lack of lay participation was singled out as the major weakness of the CCMR strategy. The report suggested, "The failure, or unwillingness, of the Coordinating Council to make the transition from a professional organization to a community organization stands out in the current evaluation as the key to both the Council's successes and failures. It continued to make contributions to the effectiveness of the professional community, but, for the most part, was frustrated in bringing about action within the larger community" (p. 66).

This analysis, however, leaves an important question unanswered, namely, why ARC received such heavy criticism from some CCMR members when ARC, which had lay membership, presumably had the structure that these same critics thought was necessary for the CCMR. We suggest that the major weaknesses of CCMR and the heavy criticism of ARC within the CCMR developed because a competitive situation evolved between ARC and some members of the CCMR, even though ARC maintained membership. In the view of many of the people interviewed, ARC was the most important actor in the mental retardation field in the San Francisco area. It was at an ARC function that the project grant upon which the CCMR was operating was first suggested, and ARC had had the first option to apply for the grant. ARC probably did not apply for the grant because it recognized its own limitations as a community interest group. The one thing ARC lacked was a mechanism for being directly influential in local public and private agencies. The CCMR, from all indications, was intended to become that mechanism. When members of the CCMR refused to accept that role and attempted to take actions which were competitive with ARC, the parents group either withdrew support or actively sought to curtail CCMR actions. This competition included controversies both between ARC and public agencies on the board and between ARC and other private, voluntary agencies with lay membership, like the Recreation Center for the Handicapped.

Another source of conflict within the CCMR was the roles of the board and the staff. As mentioned previously, the board and the staff were much the same. As a consequence, the board continuously interfered with the staff, resulting in a high turnover and serious hampering of the implementation of services since there was no consistent and sustained drive by the same staff leaders toward any objective. Likewise, the staff-board conflict meant that a large amount of energy was dissipated in internal squabbles rather than in coherent and rational action.

Despite these problems with the CCMR, many persons whom we interviewed acclaimed the hard work and noteworthy success of the CCMR; others suggested that its existence retarded rather than stimulated growth in services by "keeping people cozy for five years." Nevertheless, all agreed that it provided the first opportunity for professionals in the field of mental retardation to get to know one another and that it provided communication channels for the solution of difficult problems with individual cases. In the yearly evaluations that the CCMR made of itself and in interviews with members, the need for specific goals and for muscle to accomplish them was emphasized. A number of informants placed blame on the funding agency for not supervising the use of the grant money closely and not insisting on feasible goals. Furthermore, several participants in the CCMR, looking back over the five years, suggested that it operated more effectively before the grant was given.

They said that it received "too much money," that it "choked on money," or that "money corrupted a social group with a cause."

However, an analysis of the CCMR as a voluntary, professional association indicates that it was not only the amount of money but the type of organization which constrained the CCMR in bringing about changes in services for the mentally retarded. The tasks with which it might have been successful were obstructed by the internal conflicts among members, and the tasks around which there was a degree of consensus were too extensive for a professional association.

Routinization Stage

As the federal grant came to an end in 1970, the CCMR was trying to decide what directions it should take, if any, in the future. Under encouragement of its president Pearl Starkey, the CCMR requested affiliate status with the San Francisco Comprehensive Health Planning Council (CHPC) and eventually merged with the CHPC, with an almost new function and structure. It became the Developmental Disabilities Committee of the Health Services Task Force of CHPC. Under the new structure, the Developmental Disabilities Committee has two main objectives: health planning and review of federal grants in the field of developmental disabilities applied for by local agencies. The most important difference between the old council and the new committee is that the new committee must include other disabilities and plan for them cooperatively. As part of an ongoing organization with specific tasks, personnel, and independent funding, the association is no longer, as one interviewee put it, "firmly implanted in mid-air."

The carryovers from the CCMR are specifically the Information and Referral Service, the case committee (both currently under the Community Mental Health Mental Retardation Program), and the *Coordinator*. During the life of the project, the council produced a transportation plan for service to the handicapped and the county plan for service to the retarded in preparation for the Lanterman Act. In addition, the council supported legislation on zoning (AB 2406) and guardianship (SB 1159) and claimed to be influential in the passing of the Lanterman Act (AB 225); it also kept its members informed of other legislation concerning retardation. Participants in the association suggest that the CCMR had many unmeasurable effects, including a deeper awareness in the community of the problems of the retarded in San Francisco and a general increase in services to the retarded in the local community. Without doubt, changes of this sort did take place during the 1960s, but it is difficult to assess how much of this change was a result of changes in the environment during that period (federal, state, and local), how much was a result of the efforts of other local agencies (members or nonmembers of the CCMR), and how much occurred primarily because of the CCMR.

The expectations of former members for the newly created Developmental Disabilities Committee were still vague at the writing of this chapter. Many were concerned with the possibility of losing impetus while the committee attempted to fill out its staff with members from other disability areas. Nevertheless, most of the members who planned to continue participation felt themselves more at home planning than acting. All were hopeful that under the new direction and new structure, the problems of confused goals and internal conflict would be resolved. All felt, in addition, that their experience and training as part of the CCMR would be invaluable to the new committee.

In sum, the San Francisco project was most successful in its efforts to *coordinate information,* but it did little to *coordinate resources.* The project did try to create *cooperation* at the client level through case-management efforts. And it also tried to increase the *comprehensiveness* of programs.

3

Parents Group: Bridgeport

In Bridgeport, Connecticut, the demonstration grant was sponsored by a parents group, the Parents and Friends of Mentally Retarded Children of Bridgeport. Bridgeport is an average city, with a population of 157,000. Like Cleveland, it has a diverse ethnic population and a sizable black population. It is also an industrial city. Unlike either Cleveland or Milwaukee, Bridgeport is part of an urban sprawl that stretches along most of southern Connecticut. As a consequence, the city is both more urban and more provincial than one would expect from its size. It is more urban in that it has many of the same problems that larger cities have; it is more provincial in that it lacks a variety of organizations since the surrounding communities often specialize in particular areas.

If the Cleveland project (see Chapter Six) is a classic example of what a traditional community-organization approach can do, this project illustrates another characteristically American strategy, the efficacy of the private interest group which relies mainly on volunteer effort and contributions. What makes the Bridgeport group different from the typical interest group is that it became a service organization, offering a wide variety of programs. Many parents groups offer some services, usually transportation or leisure activities, for retarded children; but few of them build a development center and in addition operate residential-care homes, sheltered workshops, a diagnostic clinic, and a wide range of other programs. Some of the reasons for this exceptional effort need to be explored. But it still remains questionable whether one interest group, even a highly motivated and dynamic group like the one in Bridgeport, can create and coordinate a delivery system involving many organizations. One essential reason is the inherent conflict between the interests of parents and the interests of professionals, which makes cooperation between a parents organization and professional organizations difficult.

Awareness Stage

Early in the 1950s, several parents, foremost among them a remarkable woman named Evelyn Kennedy, decided to try to do something for retarded children in Bridgeport. In 1951, they formed an association, the Parents and Friends of Mentally Retarded Children of Bridgeport. As soon as the association was founded, it secured the cooperation of the superintendent of schools and established the first class in New England for the training of mentally retarded children. In the following decade, the program was expanded to include nine classes.

In the next few years, emphasis was placed on recreation and day care. First, the association persuaded the board of recreation to start a program in the evening. Then, in 1954, the association bought land and built a community center for retarded children; in 1956, an executive director and a nursery school instructor were hired for the community center. During the next few years, the association established and staffed a diagnostic clinic. By 1960, the staff of the clinic included a pediatrician, a psychologist, a psychiatrist, a psychiatric social worker (paid), a dentist, two psychometricians, a speech therapist, several social workers, and medical specialists. Also by 1960, the association had developed the following additional programs and services: preschool day care for ages three to nine, junior day care for ages three to fourteen, senior day care for ages fourteen and older, a vocational rehabilitation and sheltered workshop for ages sixteen and over, a speech therapy program, and a religious education program, one for each major faith. In addition to these services, most of which were run by volunteers (usually parents who were members of the association), several joint programs with service organizations had been developed. Members of the association even became involved in research activity and in lobbying for the mentally retarded at the state level. Largely because of their lobbying efforts, a state office for the mentally retarded was established in 1960. Several years later, Connecticut created regional centers throughout the state.

With this momentum and dynamism, the association looked to accomplish even more. It decided that it needed a much larger building as a community center to house its expanding services. The city of Bridgeport agreed to lease the land at one dollar per year, the federal government contributed $100,000 under the Hill-Burton Act, and the association raised another $300,000, hired an architect, and built the Kennedy Center. As the construction was being finished, the association applied for and received a grant from the Vocational Rehabilitation Administration (VRA), starting in 1964.

Such activities are a classic demonstration of what private initiative can accomplish when aroused. But why was this particular parents group so dynamic? It would be difficult to answer this question without doing a study of parents groups in each of the five communities. But several factors appear to be worth exploring. One key factor is that many of the parents involved were not just middle-class but upper-middle-class people with leadership and organizational skills and with access to industrialists, legislators, and others in key decision-making positions. In addition, this parents group was tightly knit; in the other urban communities, especially Los Angeles and Cleveland, one sees the fractionalization of parents groups, usually over goals. Again, a core group of about sixteen parents remained in the association throughout the entire thirteen years prior to the application for the VRA grant; the key executive positions were passed around among these individuals, and they saw each other socially. In larger cities, where there are more mental retardates, the parents are likely to be more heterogeneous; as a result, the associations might split along particular social lines as well as over different ideas as to what should be done. Then, too, it is hard to beat success. The association had accomplished a great deal and was receiving a great deal of publicity. These successes naturally reinforced the motivation and participation of the members, holding them together over a relatively long period of time.

What accounts for the innovativeness of this particular parents group? A core member of the association in the 1950s was the editor of *Children Limited,* the newspaper for the National Association for Retarded Children. In this capacity, he became a communications link with other groups all over the nation (see Orzack, Charland, and Halliday, 1969). Another important but admittedly intangible factor was the continual reinforcement of success in the many projects undertaken by the association. Each time a parent identified a need and the members agreed to it, the association was successful in obtaining its objective. This not only maintained the enthusiasm of the members, but it created an openness to innovative ideas and proposals. The members took pride in innovations and enjoyed the publicity that the association received. This taste for change, which is distinctive in the Bridgeport association, was to have consequences for the project itself.

Initiation Stage

Just after the Kennedy Center was completed, in 1964, the association received a demonstration grant from the VRA. The intent of the federal project, as reported in the July 1967 progress report (p. 1), was "to develop a model or plan of *comprehensive services* based upon the resources of the *community* and to show that the development of such comprehensive community-based services is the logical and most effective way of achieving a 'spectrum of opportunity' for the retarded individual. An immediate effect will be a vastly greater range of *vocational goals and aspirations for the retarded*." What is particularly interesting about this goal is that Bridgeport, perhaps more than any other project, did initially want to develop cooperative relationships with other agencies. In addition, the association submitted a list of concrete proposals, projects identified by the parents as needs for their children. And here we see one of the great strengths of client representation in shaping organizational goals. The parents had day-to-day observations of what their children needed and, as a consequence, recognized needs that might be missed by professionals.

Implementation Stage

Structural changes. Essentially, the demonstration project resulted in the addition of a new service organization to the board of a voluntary association. Prior to the demonstration grant, the Parents and Friends were in essence a board with an executive director who supervised the few paid staff members. When the project was started with funds from the demonstration grant, a new position was created—namely, project director. This person reported not to the executive director but directly to the board and, more specifically, to the grant committee. The hiring of the professional staff and the development of programs were largely in the hands of the project director. A dual authority structure was created since the project director reported to the board of the Parents and Friends, who were not social-service professionals, and not to the executive director, who was a professional. Such dual authority structures are inherently conflictive, for it is inevitable that disagreement over a policy or other issue will arise between the board and the executive director. In such a situation it is highly probable, if not inevitable, that the person in the role of project director will want to aggrandize his role vis-à-vis the board. For a wide variety of reasons, the project director gradually became the de facto executive director. He was well experienced in the field of mental retardation, whereas the executive director was not. His personality encouraged others to seek advice from him. Gradually the board realized this and requested the resignation of the executive director. However, the project director refused to be de jure executive director when the position was offered to him. Again, the desire was to maintain the complete separation of the project from the association. As a consequence, a staff member was appointed to fill the position, but the project director functioned as both executive director and project director. A further change occurred in the structure in 1965, when the new Kennedy Center was absorbed by the state. Since most of the day-care centers, previously supervised by the executive director, were taken over at that time, the role of the executive director was further diminished.

The informal relationships changed as well. In 1965 a new board president was elected and a new clinical director appointed. The new president, who was also a professional, began to work in close liaison with the project director, so that many decisions appropriately belonging to the executive director were now made by the project director and the president. To make matters even more complicated, the new clinical director, recruited from mental health, felt that his program deserved autonomy not only from the board but also from the project director. Thus, the power struggle became a three-sided one. But the major problem was that the board wanted to be executive director and maintain tight control. As a consequence, the duties of the executive director were never more than public relations and some administration.

Operation of Kennedy Center. Much of the grant money in the first year was used to run the newly opened Kennedy Center. Quickly, within the first year, the operation proved to be much more expensive and demanding than had been realized. In 1965, the association offered to donate the center to the state so that it could become one of the regional centers authorized in prior legislation. Connecticut accepted and agreed also to accept the outstanding mortgage of $75,000. In the same legislation, two other regional centers were authorized. As part of the arrangement, the state also absorbed the day-care programs. Some of the staff that had been in them went to work for the state. When the sale of the Kennedy Center was completed, the offices of the association and the project were combined in the same facility.

New programs. In addition to getting the Kennedy Center started, the project also began to operate two residential-care units, one for boys and one for older girls, staffed by house parents. Another new program, the Tri-Us program for the severely retarded, provided training in personal hygiene, simple household tasks, and shopping. Some of the trainees even progressed to doing simple maintenance work at low-cost projects. This program was funded by a grant from the Public Health Service.

The new project director and the new professional staff attempted to move in two directions. First, they tried to place certain services in other organizations and agencies; for example, they developed a swimming program with the YMCA. But some of the parents did not like the idea of others' taking care of their children; that is, they resented any move from a parent-oriented program to a professional one. Second, the project director and his staff attempted to include other mentally retarded children—that is, clients other than the children of the parents involved in the association—in various programs. Again, this caused a great deal of friction.

Period of conflict. In the space of just one year, the latent conflicts between the professionals and the parents became manifest. Much of the conflict centered on whether services should be turned over to other agencies and whether other children should be brought in. But the major upheaval occurred over the role of professionals in a highly emotional area, the participation of children in the sheltered workshop. When the project director and the workshop director attempted to exclude some of the severely retarded children from the workshop, the parents whose children were affected objected strenuously and vocally.

Then, when the project director began exploring the possibility of forming an independent association, the parental-professional conflict reached climactic proportions. The executive director and the project director were asked to resign. The president of the board resigned in protest. The workshop director and about half the professional staff also left in sympathy. The vice-president was acting president until a new executive director was found six months later. But the ambiguities of the position of the executive director remained. The new one lasted about one year and his replacement only two years. There were four directors in the five years of the demonstration grant, and for two six-month periods there was no executive director at all.

Analysis of Strategy

Displacement of goals. The original objectives were to develop comprehensive services built largely upon local resources. To achieve these objectives, the project director tried to create cooperative relationships with other organizations, transferring programs where possible. Also the staff tried to involve additional retarded children in the programs. Once the parents saw the consequences of these goals and the means used to achieve them, they resented being eliminated from certain volunteer activities and losing control. As the conflict between parents and professionals became manifest, the real objectives of the parents became clear. Most of them did not want to reach out in the community or to expand existing services if thereby they would lose their control over these services and programs. They wanted their own children to receive a great deal of care and attention. Thus, after the first project director resigned, little more was done in the way of reaching out into the community or even in developing a comprehensive program of services.

Causes of conflict. At the outset of the demonstration project, eight or nine professionals were hired in addition to the previous staff. Soon staff-board conflicts developed. Previously, both the parents and the professionals felt that they had essentially the same objectives: to develop a continuum of care and to provide quality services for the mentally retarded. But parents and professionals have different views of specific goals and of the means to achieve them. In most situations, these conflicts and differences in perspectives are never made manifest. The parents are separated in their association, and the professionals are somewhat protected in their service organizations. Here, the professionals worked for the parents and therefore these fundamental differences quickly became apparent.

What are these inherent differences? The first fundamental difference centers around the emotional involvement in the client. For the professional, the mentally retarded child is a client, and each is worthy of the same attention. For the parent, the client is his child and his child deserves special consideration and attention. Whether or not one calls this a conflict between universalistic and particularistic standards (Parsons, 1951), it is fundamental and is unlikely to be easily resolved because each perspective is structurally determined by the nature of the relationship with the child. From this difference flow a number of policy conflicts that did in fact occur in the Bridgeport project. The parents wanted to continue to provide their volunteer services, whereas the professionals in some instances felt that the parents should be replaced by specially trained personnel. Moreover, the professionals wanted to expand the number of clients and turn certain programs over to other agencies; the parents wanted to keep their programs and not to expand the number of children being served. In short, professionals are interested in expanding their client populations, especially since expansion brings not only more business but more funds; parents are interested in preventing a dilution of the services to their own children.

The second source of conflict concerned the use of parent volunteer services. The sudden intrusion of professionals in some of these areas was bound to create conflict, especially since the professionals wanted to transfer some of the services to other organizations. To eliminate opportunities to provide volunteer work meant striking at one of the basic pillars of a volunteer association. However, the participation of volunteers in a professionally run organization involved the visibility of professional activities and, if they occurred, of errors or poor judgment on the part of professionals. Thus, on the one hand, professionals complained about the intrusion of parents; on the other hand, parents complained about the problems that occurred when the professionals assumed control.

The third source of conflict centered around the extent of control the board could exert over the professionals—the struggle between lay (or committee) control and professional autonomy. A volunteer association such as the Friends and Parents, being tight-knit, was particularly sensitive to what the parents wanted. The long hours of volunteer work were rewarded by an attentive and demanding board. In fact, being on an active board that carefully supervised the work of the agency was itself an important reward. Thus, the tighter supervision of this board is understandable. Likewise the demands of professionals for autonomy are well known.

Another factor affecting the conflict between professionals and parents was the rapid growth in size of the professional staff. The demonstration grant resulted in a doubling of staff size. Indeed, generally, a demonstration grant probably should not be funded when the amount of money for salaries is more than a 25 percent increase in a one-year period. Under these circumstances of rapid increase in both personnel and activities, the opportunities for integration of the professionals and the parents were limited. Particularly with a tightly knit, homogeneous, and stable board, as was Bridgeport's, it would have been better to add staff members one by one. Perhaps the creation of board-staff committees might provide a communications link that would result in more understanding of each perspective—professional and parental.

Although it is much less certain and more conjectural, one suspects that another source of conflict was different social-class interests. The association had few members of the working class, whose children perhaps deserved more intensive treatment because they had more serious disabilities. The children of its members had much lower incidence of mental retardation, and they desired intensive treatment and care for their children. If the services became more comprehensive, they would be open to a great many working-class children. No member ever verbalized this complaint, but one suspects that the conflict over how many clients should be handled is essentially a class conflict, with the professionals representing the interests of the unrepresented clients.

Another key problem illustrated by the Bridgeport study

is the undesirability of a dual authority structure. The temptation to add projects—especially when they involve different technologies, in this instance client services as opposed to fund raising—is great. The power struggle that ensued was inevitable. Not unexpectedly, the professional project director won: he had control over most of the new staff members and the money and thus could in a figurative sense outvote the executive director. The creation of the dual authority structure was, however, itself a sign of the board's desire to keep tight control over operations and of the project director's desire to escape this control. In point of fact, it proved to be only a temporary solution to the problem of board control. In the long run, a better integration of professionals and parents than is likely with a separate or dual authority structure is necessary in such a demonstration project to produce satisfactory results.

Is there any resolution to this basic conflict? Clearly, the dual authority structure did not solve the problem. Even though the project director tried to gain autonomy, he was unable to do so. Given the nature of voluntary associations, especially dynamic and successful ones, there will be an active board if there is any association at all. If it is composed entirely of parents, then this kind of professional-client representative conflict is inevitable. Perhaps if the new project director had in the beginning carefully negotiated the role of the professional and the role of the parent, the inherent conflicts of interest would have become manifest and could have been dealt with more straightforwardly. These are real conflicts of interest, but if the structure allows for continued dialogue the conflicts can at least be managed. Lawrence and Lorsch (1967) suggest mechanisms that can help to handle these conflicts. In this specific case, the executive director should have functioned as an intermediary between the professionals and the parents. Another crucial mechanism would be joint staff-parent committees and staff participation in the board meetings.

Can these problems that seem to be inherent in board control of a professional director and staff be avoided if a parents group is the sponsor of such a project? It seems unlikely unless the parents group is willing to accept nonparent members

on the board. Given the success of this particular group, its high
solidarity, and its experiences in organizational management, it
seems unlikely that this was a possibility in Bridgeport. The Parents and Friends would be unwilling to accept new board members because they would be seen as outsiders. What they might
have been willing to accept were board committees with staff
members. If so, then new communication links would have been
established between the parents groups and the professionals,
which, in turn, would have helped to acquaint both groups with
the perspectives of others.

This is a basic and fundamental organizational problem.
Parental boards are most successful when the task involves fund
raising and public relations. As soon as services are developed
and professionals recruited, an inherent struggle is likely to
occur. However, boards without parents run the risk of ignoring
the needs of clients defined as important by parents. It is in
recognition of this fact that states such as California are experimenting with community boards that have little actual power
but still can influence the structuring of the delivery system.
Another possible arrangement might provide for a certain proportion of parents on a board that also has sufficient power to
control a range of services for the mentally retarded.

Factors affecting implementation of services. A major
factor affecting implementation was obviously the conflict
between staff and board. The resulting turnover and lack of
stability in executive leadership meant that several years or
more of the project were consumed by conflicts and their after-
math—start-up time for new personnel, working out new organizational arrangements, and the like. Indeed, given these difficulties, it is amazing that the Tri-Us program, the one new
program created in the latter years of the project, was success-
fully launched at all.

Although conflict can have a number of advantages, when
it reaches too high a level it tends to produce an apathetic after-
effect: no one wants to do anything, in part because of emotional exhaustion. Several of the key personnel in the association were thinking of leaving at the time we did the study. The
reasons were many, but clearly the association had lost its élan.

There were no more successes. There were not even any new initiatives. Innovation and inspiration had become the victims.

The long-term consequences of the inherent conflicts and the inability to resolve them were seen in the continual change of executive directors. More important, the person sought became less and less a professional. At the time we finished our study, the association had decided to hire one of the office secretaries as executive director. Needless to say, this degree of fear of professional control cannot be helpful for program innovation or the creation of a dynamic organization. The continual success of the association during the late 1950s and early 1960s had acted as a catalyst, encouraging the members to develop new problems and broaden their horizons. The massive upheaval of the agency had the exact opposite consequence. For once the association experienced a failure, which discouraged new efforts. The source of the conflict appeared to be the new professionals who had arrived with new programs. Therefore, the solution was to eliminate not only the professionals but any new programs that would require the hiring of them. Yet, this remained the main area of need and the obvious place for future expansion. Because much of the conflict had occurred over innovative ideas, the interest in change in general and in specific programs in particular became less. The association stopped trying. In the words of one staff member, "If the federal government were to offer us a million dollars to help the kids, they [the parents in the association] would turn it down." In short, no more implementation of services, especially ones that required professionals.

Another factor affecting implementation was the desire of the board and the parents in general to remain involved in the services that were currently being provided. This desire to maintain current programming eliminated any attempt at coordinating services. Unfortunately, the energy of the parents was not directed toward developing new services and new volunteer activities since they clearly did recognize what was needed.

Another, more intangible, factor was the gradual loss of élan of the board for reasons other than the conflict. The same leaders had been involved in the organization for ten to fifteen years as the project was coming to an end. A loss of momentum is inevitable after such a long period of time. Over time, leaders are likely to become more concerned with consolidating previous activities and innovations rather than breaking new ground. Yet, because of the nature of this leadership—tightly knit, relatively homogeneous, and successful—a large turnover of board membership was prevented. As a consequence, there was little circulation of members on the board. When the crisis occurred, it was a relatively new member of the board who quit and not one of the leaders of long standing. Concomitant with these changes, and reflecting them, was the choice of executive directors. Each new director was less interested in developing programs—understandably so, given the history of the previous conflict. So, in effect, a cycle of consolidation, retrenchment, and retreat reinforced itself during the last years of the grant.

Routinization Stage

As the federal grant came to an end, the association had ceased to be an innovator and instead was concerned only with the maintenance of existing programs. The leaders had a clear image of where they wanted to go: no more programs, no more professionals, and no more government funds. The association had built a steady and reliable list of contributors and held its annual fund-raising campaign. There was no desire to expand in any way.

The programs started were maintained and continued. Thus, one can literally say that as a consequence of the federal grant there was routinization and not disappearance, a problem that occurred in other demonstration projects. However, one is not sure that the association will retain its members. To maintain élan requires continued success, something that was no longer occurring. At the same time, if some new leaders should appear, they might provide a new direction and a new cycle of expansion and program development.

Clearly the major thrust of this project was in the area of *coordination of programs* for those clients already being served. Much of the interest was in trying to develop a *comprehensive* list of programs. There was little concern about the *compatibility* of programs, the *coordination of resources,* or the development of *cooperation* between the professionals and the client representatives.

4

Private Organization:
Milwaukee

In Milwaukee, Jewish Vocational Service (JVS) was the sponsor of the demonstration grant funded by the Vocational Rehabilitation Administration (VRA). This project differed from the others in that it was designed as an experiment; it was under the auspices of a private agency; and, most important, an entirely different structure—a coalition of organizations—evolved. The history of the project falls into two general periods: the operation of the demonstration project, called Structured Community Services (SCS); and the development and operation of a coalition of organizations, the Agencies Integrated Delivery Services (AIDS).

From 1960 to 1970, the Milwaukee Standard Metropolitan Statistical Area (Milwaukee County) grew only from 1,300,000 to 1,400,000. Approximately 90 percent of this total is urban. The percentage of blacks increased from 9 to 15 percent in the city of Milwaukee itself. This black population however is relatively small, primarily the result of migration after

World War II. In general, the city was been slow to move into the various federal programs. Although it has had a socialist mayor for a good part of its history, there is still a strong conservative vote within the metropolitan area. Beyond these characteristics, Milwaukee is a typical midwestern city; it is industrial, settled, and saddled with many of the same problems faced by other older American cities.

In 1964, prior to the awarding of the demonstration grant, services for mentally retarded were dominated by three private agencies in Milwaukee: JVS, Goodwill Industries, and Curative Workshop. Goodwill was engaged primarily in work training and sheltered employment; it serviced the disabled of all categories, including the mentally retarded. The agency operated several outlet stores in which the products of its workshop were sold. Curative Workshop offered a comprehensive range of services to the disabled. One of its main divisions, the Kiwanis Children's Hospital, provided diagnostic and recreational facilities and training in basic living skills for children. Another main division offered diagnostic services, sheltered employment, work training, and psychological counseling for adults. This organization was known for its innovations in servicing and programming as well as for the high professional quality of its staff. Educational services that were not part of vocational rehabilitation for the mentally retarded of school age were handled through the city public school system, by various suburban school systems in the rest of the county, and by some parochial schools. The school system provided services for moderately retarded children and for severely retarded individuals if they were ambulatory and somewhat cooperative.

Awareness Stage

The Milwaukee County Public Welfare Department came into contact with a large number of retarded but provided no specific services with the important exception of work training and foster-home placement. Perhaps because of its extensive contact with the retarded persons on its welfare rolls and its inability (because of its public mandate) to engage in the direct provision of services, the directors of this bureau realized more acutely than others the gaps in services in the community and the need for integration of those services that did exist. Another group which recognized the problem was the Department of Vocational Rehabilitation (DVR), a state agency which contracted for diagnostic services, certified an individual as disabled in some way, and then contracted with private providers for rehabilitative services. Its director was quick to point out gaps and omissions and urged that his own budget be increased so that his office could coordinate services for the mentally retarded. This agency was one of the principal sources of funds since its referrals involved the direct purchase of care. Its referral practices however were the object of endless disputes and complaints from the private agencies; each agency felt that its rivals were getting more or better-quality clients than it was.

Thus, in the early 1960s the services for the retarded in Milwaukee were relatively uncoordinated, competitive, and full of conflict and bickering. The DVR could not use its financial clout to force agencies to coordinate since they could go as a powerful lobby group to the state legislature and complain. Until 1967, when the Milwaukee County Mental Health Planning Committee was charged with planning retardation services for the community, there was no areawide planning body. The United Fund had engaged in some community planning of its own, usually compiling inventories of services and making suggestions for revision of services. In general, however, the United Fund appeals for integration of services and programs tended to be ignored by the larger service organizations since they received government funds from all levels—federal, state, county, and city—and were therefore not dependent on the United Fund.

Initiation of SCS

The VRA demonstration grant in Milwaukee was given to JVS, a private agency with a long history of service to the retarded and disabled. Besides providing diagnostic services, vocational training, and sheltered employment, JVS was also one of

the principal sources for new programs and services for the
retarded. A special project, the SCS, was set up to administer
the grant.

A private agency, even in a context less competitive than
that of Milwaukee, cannot hope to persuade its rivals to share
clients, funding, or staff (Aiken and Hage, 1968); nor do most
private agencies, once they have received a sizable grant, willingly spread this money around to their rivals. Consequently,
Michael Galazan, the director of JVS, did not attempt to organize the whole community but only to establish a miniature
continuum of care and a fixed point of referral for a limited
number of clients on an experimental basis. If such services
were shown to benefit these clients, he hoped that other
agencies would either cooperate in setting up a communitywide
system or at least develop their own miniature fixed points of
referral and continua of care.

In order to demonstrate the usefulness of service integration, the project used the following method. Two groups—
experimental and control—of five hundred retarded were selected. All were given an assessment (a medical, social, and
psychological diagnosis) paid for by the DVR to determine their
degree of retardation and their level of functioning. For a five-
year period, the experimental group participated in a series of
programs designed to fill the gaps in the continuum of care.
Clients in the experimental group were assigned to specially
trained case coordinators, who examined their histories, recommended to other agencies a proper sequence of services, referred
the clients to these agencies, and then followed their progress.
The project itself did not engage in the direct delivery of services. At the end of the five-year period, a measure was taken of
both groups to see whether the experimental group had improved more than the control. JVS hoped to show sufficient
differences between the experimental and control groups so
that the community would be well aware of the advantages of
an integrated delivery system and would therefore provide support to continue the project and gradually expand the number
of clients—until, eventually perhaps, all the retarded in the area
might be included in the program of services.

Success in case coordination depended heavily on referral of cases by other organizations. From the beginning, however, the project was hampered in its efforts to deal with these organizations because of its ties to its sponsor, JVS. Everyone in the welfare community of Milwaukee knew that the project was planned, organized, and staffed almost entirely within JVS. Since no one perceived the project as autonomous of the sponsor, it was inseparably linked with JVS, becoming in the process subject to the same reactions, suspicions, and competition that focused on the sponsoring agency. In addition, only after initiation of the project, when the goals and methods had already been spelled out, were the other rehabilitation organizations in the community notified of its nature and intent. Given the rivalry and competition among the major mental retardation service agencies in the community, such late notification was not likely to reduce interagency competition (although services for clients may never have been developed had all the competitors planned the services in advance).

Change strategy. One strategy used to elicit participation once the project had been announced was the establishment of an advisory committee composed of high-level representatives from the major agencies providing services for the retarded. In this way, the project was to be legitimized as a community-sponsored undertaking. This advisory group, composed of about twenty-six people, was called the Participating Agencies Advisory Committee. It met regularly in the JVS building during the project. Despite moderate to good attendance, however, it failed to drum up support for project undertakings. Participants in retrospect claimed that it accomplished little (the minutes of the meetings support this claim). Most complained that decisions were made in the project and by JVS, not in the committee. Consequently, even though it brought many people together who otherwise seldom met, the committee did not confer upon the project legitimacy as a community enterprise, primarily because its functions were limited largely to advice and not policy.

As a second strategy to enhance the image of the project, great pains were taken in selecting the director to ensure that he or she measured up to the highest professional standards, standards which were somewhat above those of the sponsoring agency. Generally, however, these efforts went unnoticed. An alternative strategy might have been to put on the staff personnel of several agencies besides the sponsor. JVS might have gained some legitimacy with this procedure as well as providing a valuable communications link. (See the Los Angeles project, Chapter Five, for an example of this technique.)

One other strategy, the sharing of funds by JVS, was tried in a limited way with two small programs. But the amount of the funds and time for which they were shared were insufficient to make the cooperating agency dependent on the program.

Goals. Galazan felt that the ideal continuum of care for the individual would include evaluation, medical treatment, day care, educational services, work adjustment, placement, sheltered employment, and recreational opportunities. Although some agencies provided some of these services for particular age groups, there were great gaps, especially for preschool youngsters, for adults not properly referred after high school, and for many adults who either were never referred at all or had been dropped out of one program and never picked up by another. To fill these gaps an information and referral service with a follow-up procedure was needed since there was no fixed point at which a retarded person's case history was collected and to which each retarded client could return if necessary. A major objective of the SCS project was the creation of such a service. The person who handled the case at the fixed point (the case coordinator) would know the history of the client and would act as an advocate for him in obtaining the needed services.

Implementation of SCS

Structure. The organizational arrangement of the SCS project was determined largely by its ties to JVS. The staff of the project reported directly to the board of JVS. No respondents recalled that this board ever significantly curtailed the project in its activities. The Participating Agencies Advisory

Committee also received reports from the staff of the project as well as from the executive director of JVS. During its five years of operation, the project itself had several directors and between eleven and twelve staff members, depending on the number of programs being conducted at the time. Some of these staff persons acted on a consulting basis; others had only half-time appointments with the project. Project staff were recruited primarily from the staff of the sponsoring agency and consisted largely of professional social workers, the major exception being the first directors of the project. Since the project was housed within JVS, it could tap its resources whenever the need arose and so was able to obtain other forms of professional service and advice. Several specialists were brought in from the community. Most notably, a specialist from the University of Wisconsin-Madison was largely responsible for the experimental design of the project and of many of its programs. After the second year the project was able to augment its staff with four case coordinators from its own training program.

The influence of the sponsoring agency upon the SCS project went beyond the official relationship between the SCS director, the JVS director, and the advisory committee. In its five-year history the SCS project had five directors. The first two were hired from outside JVS; the last three were former members of the JVS staff. For the second year the SCS project had no director; Galazan filled in and appointed one of his staff to handle the administrative details. The SCS directors were hand picked by Galazan. He also signed and helped prepare the budget and certified annual progress reports and requests for funding continuation.

Coordinating information and cases. Since the project was to demonstrate continuum of care and fixed point of referral, it had to know at the outset what services were available to the retarded. Consequently, one of its first tasks was to develop a directory of community services. All agencies responded eagerly and rapidly to the idea of a directory. Unfortunately, however, the questionnaire used to gather information lent itself to many inaccuracies: agencies tended to exaggerate the extent of their services, to suggest that a wider variety of pro-

grams were open to retarded clients than were, and to overesti-
mate the number of clients being served and referred by them.
Since the project staff did not take the time to conduct site
visits (assuming that such checks would have been allowed),
inaccuracies and distortions invariably crept into the directory.

The project also needed information on the number of
retarded in the community, the exact nature of their disabilities, and the services provided to them. Here, however, the rival
agencies were not cooperative. While no one openly charged
that the sponsoring agency would use this information to obtain
more clients, distrust, suspicion, and disagreement plagued the
registry from the outset. Some claimed labeling problems
("Who can say who is mentally retarded? Any mistakes here
would be made permanent by a registry"), professional ethics,
and confidentiality ("Who knows what this new staff will do
with our information?"). The city school system refused to
divulge any information because of "school board policy."
Some agencies did provide coded lists; but since the coded list
from one agency could not be compared with lists from another
(so that, for instance, it was impossible to learn whether the
same client was being served by two agencies) and since few parents of retarded children volunteered to participate in the project, the registry was not accurate. Of the estimated 33,000
retarded in the area, only 9000 were ever registered; and some
of these must have been duplicates.

In addition to obtaining information from other agencies,
the project also had to be sure that those agencies offered good
service to a client, offered him new programs, or referred him
elsewhere for more appropriate services. However, such procedures were not even attempted by the project staff—probably
because they knew that such attempts would be futile. Approximately four hundred of the five hundred clients in the experimental group were monitored, but this monitoring frequently
resulted in little more than a recording of the services a client
was given.

Documenting needs. A survey by the SCS staff showed
that the retarded population was especially lacking in services in
four areas: medical services, family counseling, mental health

services, and legal services. In the area of medical services the problems found were those one would expect. The retarded had access problems, frequently could not understand why they should follow a doctor's regimen, and did not have sufficient resources to pay for medical services. The story was much the same with mental health services. Organizations tended to neglect the retarded, concentrating instead on other groups in the population. Similarly, the family-counseling services of most agencies tended not to include the retarded population; when they did handle such clients, they frequently failed to give them the special handling their disabilities required. During the third and fourth year, the SCS analyzed the problems of the mentally retarded offender. An analysis was made of the crimes typically committed by the retarded and of the rehabilitation services needed by them.

New programs. A program for black unwed mothers was carried out in the third and fourth years of the project. Several programs also were initiated in cooperation with other agencies in the area. For example, Planned Parenthood, in cooperation with the SCS staff, undertook a small program of providing birth-control and family-planning information to a limited group of retarded. Those in this program apparently benefited from it. Because state legislation hampered continuation of this program, efforts were channeled into lobbying with the state legislature to change laws which prohibited dissemination of certain kinds of birth-control information.

In the third year of the project, employment opportunities for the retarded were analyzed; as a result, a joint program was established by the SCS project and the Youth Opportunity Center of the Wisconsin State Employment Service. This program had moderate success in improving the skill of the employment service in dealing with retarded job applicants and in finding jobs for retarded persons; however, the program was not continued beyond the period of the funding. Another program established in the third year of the project, in cooperation with the Silver Spring Neighborhood Center, attempted to develop outreach techniques for retarded persons who were socially isolated. The project provided funding, consultation, and case coordination, while the center contributed staff and space. This program, despite its success in reaching some retarded persons, was not continued when the SCS funding was terminated. A similar program to establish recreational opportunities for a small group of retarded was developed in the third and fourth years, in cooperation with Northwest YMCA. This organization supplied the space, the SCS project provided the funding, and volunteers served as the staff. The group of retarded in the program again showed some measurable improvement, but the program was terminated when the SCS project had to discontinue funding.

Three programs, however, did continue after the SCS project ceased. One, with the Jewish Community Center, provided recreational programs for severely retarded adults. Responsibility for this program was later assumed by the adult education division of the Milwaukee public school system. A comprehensive medical, psychological, and social diagnosis program for the retarded participating in the SCS project was later continued in many of the agencies in the area because the DVR saw the value of purchasing such services. Finally, the training program for case coordinators, originally developed jointly by the SCS project and the University of Wisconsin-Milwaukee, was taken over completely by the university.

Analysis of SCS Strategy

Displacement of goals. The shift in project goals may best be described as an abandonment of the original scientific design and of attempts to coordinate information and cases with other organizations. After futile attempts were made to create the registry and to coordinate cases through programs with other agencies, the project began to shift its energies to programs not dependent upon cooperation from competitors. In spite of its shift of goals, however, the project still did not engage in the direct provision of services.

From its inception, SCS took seriously the federal mandate to examine the availability of services in the community, to discover new areas in which services could be provided, and to attempt to make comprehensive care available to the retarded. Many ideas about the services needed occurred to the project staff during the first two years (1964-1965), but little could be done with this information since energies were devoted to the struggles over the registry and the assessment of the subjects selected for the experimental and control groups. When these activities were completed or when work on them terminated because of lack of community support, a new strategy for creating a comprehensive set of services was developed. The plan was to document needs and to inform other agencies of these needs, in the hope that the other agencies might expand their services. In areas in which there were especially important gaps in service and in which the project staff had expertise, a demonstration project would be established with a limited group of retarded to show that they would indeed profit from a new program. Ideally, this service would then be continued by another agency in the county.

Factors affecting implementation of services. Many reasons have been offered for the checkered history of cooperation and program implementation achieved by the SCS project. Many respondents claimed that specific problems were encountered because the project was sponsored by and located in the JVS. Informants felt that personality clashes between Galazan and others in the community who were asked to cooperate greatly hindered the project. Another source of hostility to the sponsor arose from its reputation among some other private organizations of having a less professional staff than they. Hence, agencies were reluctant to refer clients to the SCS, believing that the clients would not be as professionally treated there as in the referring agency. The sponsor took steps to staff the SCS with qualified professional personnel, but this change was not widely recognized or admitted by the other agencies.

The principal reasons other agencies did not cooperate with the project however were much more basic than professional reputations and personality conflicts. To coordinate a case with the SCS was a procedure costly in agency reputation and staff time. Since case coordination involved assessment of the quality of the services provided by an agency, case coordinators would know of deficiencies and problems. No agency willingly allows such evaluations to be made by anyone on the outside. In addition, coordination requires extensive use of staff time to properly conduct a case, to report on progress to the case coordinator, and to refer the case elsewhere if need be. These were the concrete costs which agencies readily perceived full cooperation with the SCS would entail. In addition, many feared that if their clients were referred to the SCS project, they might become clients of JVS and be lost as sources of income. Many also felt that referring clients to the SCS would only enhance the reputation of the sponsor and do nothing for that of the referring agency. In an atmosphere of rivalry, these fears were important. Indeed, if the private auspices of the project did hinder its effectiveness, it was because it gave rise to such fears.

The single most important reason for the lack of cooperation with the SCS project was the competition between the key agencies involved, specifically Goodwill and Curative. All of them received a major part of their funds from the same agency, DVR. As a consequence, each agency attempted to demonstrate the superiority of its services. This competition made the idea of case coordination particularly repugnant.

Some goals of the project did not elicit cooperation because other organizations did not see their usefulness or thought that they unnecessarily duplicated existing programs. In particular, the registry was perceived as unnecessary. People had serious reservations about listing all retarded at a central point, as previously discussed. Others felt they already provided a continuum of care through the services of their own agencies and thought, therefore, that the SCS was duplicating programs by encouraging other organizations to offer a full range. Still others thought they were the principal information source about mental retardation in the community and that the SCS information and referral efforts were duplications of their services.

Several respondents took the position that the only way the project could have achieved cooperation would have been to buy it. With several small exceptions—for example, the YMCA program mentioned above—SCS money stayed within the sponsoring organization. If the money had been farmed out to other agencies, the programs of the SCS might have been established on a permanent basis. There was some resentment about the fact that the sponsor kept all the money for itself, but most other directors felt this to be the most logical course for a good businessman to follow, implying that if they had received the grant, they would have done the same.

The argument that the project could have purchased cooperation is plausible on the surface, but two significant aspects of the funding picture during the 1960s suggest that the purchase of cooperation would have been difficult. First, the size of the grant from VRA was little more than a hundred thousand dollars per year. One could not offer to even a few agencies much inducement with this kind of a budget. Second, there was a steady increase in the amount of money available. With one major exception (in which the sponsoring agency of the project lost some of its DVR funding in 1969), there were no severe cutbacks in funds from 1964, when the SCS project began, to 1969, when the SCS grant was terminated. The dynamics here seem clear. With increasing amounts of financial resources, agencies developed new programs over which they had total control or continued old programs rather than incur the costs entailed in a truly cooperative and coordinated venture. Any agency attempting to coordinate others in affluent times will find coordination cannot simply be bought; conversely, under conditions of scarcity, agencies are more likely to sacrifice autonomy over programs in order to obtain needed resources.

The last reason for the failure to elicit cooperation is certainly not the least. The turnover in the personnel of the project definitely hindered it in establishing firm links with other agencies. In the five years of the project, SCS had five directors or acting directors. Several respondents mentioned that after they had established basic working relations with one director, they had to begin all over again with another one. This turnover also gave the impression that important decisions for the project were made by the sponsor and not by the project directors; the

project directors changed so frequently it was hard to see how
they could secure a firm grasp on policy. This turnover was
explained by respondents as the result of many factors, among
them the offer of better jobs, the transfer of husbands, and the
lack of control directors had over major policy decisions. Perhaps a more important reason was that anyone undertaking the
job of director knew his or her tenure was limited by the duration of the funding. Hence, the directorship attracted people
interested in a temporary job or people who saw the job as a
stepping stone to other employment.

It is difficult to weigh the merits of these various reasons
for the failure of the SCS to elicit cooperation. Many of them
are obviously hindsight, others a reaction to the limited success
of the AIDS project described below, and others convenient and
defensible justifications of past actions. We believe three reasons
were especially important. First, there was the auspices of the
project, although it is doubtful that any agency in Milwaukee,
public or private, would have been totally successful in such an
effort. Second, there was not enough funding to make cooperation attractive. A million dollar annual budget might have produced different results. Third, the costs in staff time and to
agency reputations resulting from case coordination were considerable. The AIDS project eliminated the problem of auspices
and did not attempt any activities of the SCS judged to be needless duplication, but it still ran into problems because of these
other costs.

Transition from SCS to AIDS

In 1968, as Galazan saw the money for the SCS project
coming to an end, he consulted with county and state officials
about the feasibility of setting up a fixed point of referral and
continuum of care in each of the three major rehabilitation
agencies (JVS, Curative Workshop, Goodwill). In this plan,
other agencies providing tangential services to the retarded
would be satellites of the big three. After the experience with
SCS, Galazan believed that the inclusion of the three competitors in one case-coordination program would be counterproduc-

tive. He felt it was in their interests to compete for clients and funds and to act as if they were self-sufficient, and that these activities would hinder referrals by them to a coordination program. Edward Hida, the county administrator of vocational rehabilitation funding, and the director of the DVR and the Milwaukee County Mental Health Planning Committee were, however, opposed to such a plan because they considered it divisive. They insisted that there be only one fixed point of referral and continuum of care in the community. In the meanwhile, JVS had applied to the federal government for a one-year extension of the five-year SCS. In the proposal, it promised to continue the continuum of care until public auspices and a cooperative agreement of service provision could be achieved, and Galazan agreed that he would lobby for these goals. His plan for the one-year extension, however, resembled the original plan, in which JVS was the only rehabilitation agency which participated. The omission of Curative Workshop and Goodwill later made it difficult to get them to participate in the AIDS program.

Galazan was good on his promise to lobby for what turned out to be the AIDS project. All but two of thirty respondents, when asked how the SCS evolved to AIDS, cited as the first reason his intensive efforts and persuasive techniques. There were other reasons, which will be discussed presently, but Galazan was the necessary catalyst.

Three major hurdles faced the extension of SCS from a five-year project to a permanent program: finding the appropriate public auspices in order to ensure legitimacy and remove the stigma associated with private auspices, persuading other organizations to participate, and persuading the county to provide funding. The first of these was the least problematic. All realized the project would have to be transferred to public auspices. JVS favored the Milwaukee County Public Welfare Department, while others favored the Milwaukee County Institutions. JVS preferred the County Public Welfare Department because it already had experience with the retarded in its foster-home program and placement services. The official relationship of the department to the county institutions was quite close and generally there was no rivalry between them. Eventually, Hida, who was the representative of the director of the county institutions, Galazan, and George Baldwin, director of county welfare, decided that Milwaukee County Institutions should have the AIDS program because they felt that this organization had a better chance than the Public Welfare Department of being funded by the federal government. Also, this county agency had better relations with the county board of supervisors than did its welfare counterpart. Finally, some felt the relief image of welfare would impede the retarded and their families from seeking help. Thus, the AIDS program was freed from private auspices, which had plagued SCS from its start and had limited its acceptance in the community.

Once the question of auspices had been resolved, the next problem was persuading other agencies to cooperate. As has been mentioned, Galazan's lobbying was a significant factor here. But, perhaps much more significant, if an agency agreed to participate, it could obtain new staff at a low cost of 15 percent of the total expense for the first year. This incentive was sufficient to bring seven agencies together as members of the AIDS program. Curative Workshop delayed for a time and had to be personally persuaded by Hida of the importance of its participation for the success of the program and of the fact that participation would benefit the agency while costing it nothing. Some feel that Curative Workshop finally decided to join the AIDS project because it feared being left out and incurring the displeasure of officials in county government whom it was earnestly courting at the time because of a desire to be part of a new medical center complex.

Initiation of AIDS

The eight participating agencies then signed a contractual agreement that stipulated they would cooperate with the AIDS program, accept clients referred from it and give them as much priority as possible, and attend staffing and evaluation meetings at which cases referred to AIDS would be analyzed and the best treatment decided on. It further stipulated that participating agencies would refer to AIDS some of their clients needing more services than they themselves could provide. In other words, they agreed to a considerable degree of control being exerted by this integrated delivery system for the mentally retarded.

Two vulnerabilities of the SCS project were avoided through this procedure. First, community support was carefully cultivated. Second, the three largest service delivery agencies were brought into the project on a contractual basis. The planning of AIDS was also done in consultation with the directors of all important agencies in the community, which was facilitated by their having been on the advisory committee for the SCS project.

The county was asked to fund AIDS as a complement to a federal staffing grant. Such a grant provides 75 percent funding of positions permitted under it for the first year, 63 percent funding for the second, and so on until the grant expires in fifty-one months. The grant is obviously intended as an incentive for development of community resources. The original grant request was for $527,550 for 125 professional positions for the contract agencies and for the director and coordinators of the AIDS program itself. This request was funded at only a 20 percent level, however, which meant that only a few of the professional positions in the agencies were supported along with those of the director and assistant director for AIDS. The key case coordinators were not funded. No one seemed to know why the grant was funded in such an apparently irrational manner. Regardless of the reason, this underfunding almost resulted in the elimination of the incentive for agencies to participate. Milwaukee County was asked to step in with limited funding for secretarial staff, office space, and overhead, while the participating agencies, some of which were already reluctant to enter fully into the project, were asked to pay the case coordinators' salaries.

Federal approval for the project (contingent on 25 percent local funding) was made in June 1969. Approval by the county then took nine months, and the project did not officially begin until September 1970. The major difficulty with the county came from the finance committee, which thought that such coordination was the responsibility of the state and did not want to set the precedent of the county's accepting it. At this point the coalition of organizations was able to act effectively as an advocacy group and bring pressure to bear on the finance committee. The committee eventually approved AIDS by a vote of five to two and subsequently the full board of supervisors approved the program by a vote of nineteen to five. This approval was for the entire fifty-one months, not just for the first year. This commitment meant that the county agreed in advance to pay almost the entire staff cost of the program in its last year. (The county has lived up to its commitment. In 1974, when federal funding ended, the county assumed full responsibility for AIDS by making its director and case managers full-time county employees and by paying other expenses of the program.)

The participating agencies were enticed both to lobby for the AIDS program with the county board finance committee and to pay the salaries of the AIDS case coordinators by the promise that this money would be reimbursed through Purchase of Care funds—a federal source of funding administered by the county. Since only six of the eight agencies were eligible for Purchase of Care funds, two did not contribute to the case coordinators' salaries.

Participants. Cooperation from the community was not perfect. Although many agencies were not asked because of the limited number of case coordinators in AIDS (their jobs would be impossible if too many agencies were involved), several agencies which were asked to participate refused. These were the district office of the DVR, Milwaukee city schools, and several family-counseling agencies. A variety of reasons were offered for their nonparticipation. The DVR argued that state law forbade its contracting with such a program, but it would cooperate if the need arose. The city schools claimed confidentiality again and that school board policy would forbid entry into such contractual relationships. Both these key agencies argued further that they did not see any function to be served by AIDS in relation to their programs. The DVR felt AIDS was just one more referral agency in a field already overloaded with them; as such, it was a waste of money. From its perspective these funds should have been given to the DVR. Thus, while AIDS is not competing with the service agencies, it is to some extent competing with DVR, which responded in a predictable fashion.

Several family-counseling agencies (Family Service, Catholic Family Service, and Lutheran Family Service) refused to participate when asked since, although they treated retarded persons through their normal services, they did not want to provide special services for any particular disability or to be identified as providing special services to the retarded. The director of the AIDS project and Galazan continued to attempt to persuade some of these agencies that the AIDS program needed them and that they should provide services to the retarded.

The eight contract agencies then are Curative Workshop, Goodwill Industries, JVS, Planned Parenthood, Easter Seal Child Development Center, Day Care Services for Children, Inc., United Association for Retarded Children, and Milwaukee Children's Hospital Special Development Clinic.

Structure. The AIDS program operates under the auspices of Milwaukee County and as such has the county supervisors' subcommittee on public welfare as its board. The project began with an executive director, assistant director, four case coordinators, and secretarial help. AIDS has an administrative and advisory committee composed of the executive director of AIDS and the directors (or their representatives) of the eight participating agencies. This committee meets periodically to determine policy and operating procedures for AIDS.

Goals. The basic goals of the AIDS program are to provide case coordination and a fixed point of referral for the mentally retarded. Implied in these goals are a continuum of care and a central file which clients, their families, and other agencies serving them may consult to avoid duplication of intake procedures and diagnosis. A concrete description of case-coordination activities illustrates how these goals are met. A client referred to AIDS is assigned to one of the case coordinators, who collects all available material or obtains additional diagnoses of the client's physical, psychological, and social disabilities. When these results are known, a staffing and evaluation committee meeting, attended by a multidisciplinary staff drawn from the personnel of the participating agencies, is held. This committee reviews the case, identifies needs, and recommends treatment. A client accepted for service by AIDS is considered a client of all participating agencies. One of the agencies usually assumes responsibility for the direct management of the case and commits itself to service the client with top priority. If none of the agencies can handle the case, it is referred elsewhere in the community by the case coordinator, who keeps searching until an appropriate program is found. Once treatment begins, the case coordinator follows the case closely, monitors the client's progress monthly, aids the client in finding alternative service if he completes or is dropped from a program, provides for communication between all agencies working on the case, and, when service is terminated, checks with the client periodically to determine whether additional service is needed. If any problems arise in the course of treatment, the case coordinator may convene a staffing meeting and plan new programs for the client.

Implementation of AIDS

The AIDS budget is $90,050 per year. An additional $33,695 per year pays the case coordinators' salaries. The county continues to supply space, secretaries, and its share of the director's and his assistant's salaries. The eight participating agencies continue to pay their share of the case coordinators' salaries, and all retain the professional positions which they received through AIDS. AIDS and these professional positions were funded by a federal staffing grant at a 75 percent level for the first year, 63 percent the next, and 30 percent the next. Forty-five percent of the increasing local share is paid through Purchase of Care funds.

After two years of operation, AIDS was coordinating the cases of approximately 180 clients. At this point, it stopped accepting new referrals except in emergencies in order to concentrate on the clients it had. By the end of the third year and through the fourth, new referrals were again being accepted.

The AIDS case load is heaviest in the childhood and adolescent age brackets. Mental retardation is the primary disability serviced, but children under eight from backgrounds which imply a high risk of retardation are also serviced. There are no financial requirements for AIDS service, and no fee is assessed. Each agency, however, applies its standard fee schedule.

In evaluating AIDS, success is best defined as supplying a client with programs according to his needs. As of August 1972, there were 180 clients with 213 diagnosed needs unmet by services. By March 1973, forty of these needs had been met by programs, and the number of persons needing one or more services had been reduced from 180 to 100. There are no data to use in assessing the quality of services provided by the agencies, although case coordinators attempt to monitor quality frequently.

Extent of cooperation. It is difficult to measure agency cooperation with the project. This difficulty is compounded because data collected one year may not be collected the next.

AIDS collected data indicating which agencies had referred the first one hundred clients and to which agencies these clients had been sent to receive services. In addition to the eight contract organizations, three other major sources of services or funds for the retarded—the Milwaukee city public school system, the Milwaukee County Public Welfare Department, and the DVR—referred clients. Twenty-five of the one hundred clients were referred from other agencies besides these eleven. The Public Welfare Department made extensive use of AIDS both because the number of its clients dwarfs the number in any of the contract agencies and because it did not attempt on its own to provide diagnostic and case-coordination services for the retarded. The schools, however, feel they provide reasonably adequate services for the retarded of school age and so referred only four despite the large number of retarded they serve. The DVR felt from the beginning that AIDS duplicated many of its services and consequently referred no one, although its client load is comparable with that of the Public Welfare Department. Among the contract agencies, although Goodwill, Curative Workshop, and JVS have relatively similar case loads of retarded, Curative Workshop neither referred nor received any clients, Goodwill sent four and received two, and JVS used AIDS more heavily than any of the other eight participating agencies. Thus, in general, those agencies which resisted cooperation in the beginning cooperated minimally with the program.

Unfortunately, such data could not be collected for the next three years of the program. Other figures, however, indicate the same problems in eliciting cooperation. At the end of three years of operations, data on the number of AIDS clients active in programs of the eight participating agencies, the schools, the Public Welfare Department, and the DVR showed that Curative was now handling thirteen clients, while JVS was handling twenty-seven and the Milwaukee Public Schools forty-seven. As before, DVR was not involved. The pattern is largely the same as that for referrals, with the notable exception of Curative Workshop and the city schools. However, these figures do not represent cases referred by an agency but instead the cases AIDS is coordinating of clients who are receiving services from that agency.

A principal weakness of the AIDS program in eliciting cooperation is the low amount of its funding, one result of which is that the allegiance of contracting agencies remains somewhat tenuous.

Overall, the coordination service of the AIDS program is widely recognized as quite valuable by the participating agencies. From the first, it was apparent that the cases in greatest need of coordination were the multiple-problem ones—for example, children with alcoholic or retarded parents, children of unwed parentage, clients with legal problems—because the services of several agencies would have to be enlisted. Since AIDS began early to concentrate on the multiple-problem case, fulfilling a recognized need, its success in achieving cooperation was significant.

Operational problems. Throughout its history AIDS has had a problem with staff turnover because of two basic structural problems. First, the county insists on a lengthy review of the need for a vacant position before it allocates funds to fill it. Such a policy is understandable as a money-saving device, but its effect on AIDS has been most disrupting. Two half-time case-coordinator positions were empty for several months, and for the last half of the third year of the program, the director had to operate without an assistant. Second, because staff members realized that the program was not certain of continuing to receive funds, they were enticed away by more secure career opportunities. Now that the county has adopted the program and has created civil service positions for the staff, this problem should be eliminated.

Any agency attempting to elicit interorganizational cooperation must have adequate communications links with the agencies with which it deals. In general, the AIDS program has had good communications between its case coordinators and the lower-level staff of other agencies. The real problem in AIDS interagency communications occurs with higher-level staff. The policy advisory committee has met infrequently. Furthermore, some executive directors of participating agencies do not feel they are kept sufficiently informed of the activities of AIDS. During the middle of the third year of AIDS operations, the policy advisory committee met for a general gripe session, which had two results. First, the director distributed to other participants statistics of AIDS performance and generally informed them of what AIDS was doing. Some directors still do not feel these high-level communications are adequate, and the director of AIDS is working on improving them. The second major action was establishment of an outreach program, in which case coordinators from AIDS visit other agencies, meet with key staff members to explain the value of AIDS to their clients, and participate in in-service training programs and staffing meetings in these other agencies. This program has worked well and has been a source of mutual satisfaction to AIDS and the participating agencies, except when AIDS coordinators have not made a great effort to visit other agencies or when a coordinator position has fallen vacant and no contact has been made.

The principal structure for communications with other agencies in the beginning was the staffing and evaluation meetings. In these meetings, professional staff from the participating agencies met with AIDS case coordinators to plan a set of programs for a client. These meetings were held fairly regularly through the first two and one half years of the program but ended when the assistant to the director resigned. Several complaints were raised in the advisory committee that the AIDS staff was doing the planning on its own or in consultation with only a few agencies. The AIDS director has promised to reinstate the full staffing meetings, but he feels this cannot be done with all clients because participating agencies will not take the time to attend. In any case, the lack of these meetings has been a clear deficiency in AIDS communications with other agencies.

Analysis of AIDS Strategy

The contrast between the SCS strategy and the AIDS strategy is striking, and the fact that AIDS evolved from SCS does not make the comparison less interesting. The same participants were involved—executive director, organizations, leaders —and the same obstacles existed—desires for organizational autonomy, competition between agencies, fragmentation of services, varying political jurisdictions. Yet, despite the obstacles, some progress was made toward the goal of achieving a coordinated delivery system.

The second strategy had two distinguishing characteristics. First, all the major actors, public and private, city and county, including competitors, were brought together into a coalition of organizations. Most important, the organizations were brought together before any funding had been received, and thus they could participate in the planning. Such integrated planning is necessary when heads of agencies perceive themselves as equals; it allows necessary political compromises to be made, and not unexpectedly, in some cases, this procedure can produce an improved system. Second, the organizations were offered the possibility of increasing both their funding and their power vis-à-vis some of the political jurisdictions. Under these circumstances, belonging to the coalition of organizations began to outweigh nonparticipation. Concerns for organizational autonomy were not lessened, but in the total balance they weighed less heavily. (In Chapter Eight we explore some reasons why the concern for autonomy may be unfounded when the delivery system is structured as a coalition of organizations.)

Despite minor operational problems, AIDS has shown in a limited way that case coordination and a continuum of care are possible for the mentally retarded. To improve its operations, three additional components appear desirable and may be possible if sufficient community support can be enlisted. First, AIDS needs a compliance mechanism. This step was not feasible in the past because AIDS was reluctant to discipline agencies upon whose good will it depended for continued funding. But, as a county-funded program, AIDS may be able to incorporate if not a disciplinary device at least an incentive system for cooperation. It would be contradictory from the county point of view to pay for a coordinating mechanism which relies only on persuasion.

Second, AIDS needs more case coordinators. Four case coordinators currently carry about 240 clients. Presumably, they could increase their output and handle more cases, but even if they double their case load, many cases will still be in need of coordination and many will have to be turned away because of insufficient manpower.

Third, AIDS should review the quality of service. This function would be most controversial, but, again, the county might be sold such an idea for reasons of accountability. Each year, the county dispenses millions in its own and state and federal monies to the service agencies for retardation, and yet, outside of cost-accounting procedures, there is no review of the quality of care they are purchasing or funding. The trick here would be to get private agencies to accept such a review. Some are clearly interested; some intend to request it; but others are quite likely to do everything they can to sabotage a program empowered to investigate and make judgments on the quality of their services.

Routinization Stage

The federal staffing grant which funded the AIDS program expired in March 1974. AIDS was reviewed by the Milwaukee County Mental Health Planning Committee, and the recommendation was for continued funding by the county, which was granted. It is most difficult to predict at this point whether AIDS will be continued indefinitely by the county. There are simply too many contingencies. Some agency directors may not come to AIDS' rescue because of deficiencies in AIDS communications links with them. Much work remains to be done in courting their favor, in informing them of the value of AIDS, and in persuading them to lobby for it—all without a firm foundation of good relations at this point. But other problems are perhaps more serious if AIDS is to enlist the support of even the most friendly agencies. First, referring clients to AIDS has meant the cost of staff time and the exposure of shortcomings in services to outsiders. Second, the participating agencies do not receive additional staff positions from the county, one of the key incentives of the original AIDS program.

However, the lower-level staff members of the participating agencies are fairly unanimous in their approbation of the job AIDS can do for their multiple-problem clients. With improved communications, this benefit is also becoming clear to the executive directors of the participating organizations and may help in eliciting their support. More important, the support of Hida, the county administrator of Purchase of Care funds, Title I funds, Day Care monies, state grants-in-aid, and several other federal, state, and local forms of funding, is significant. He is an avid supporter of AIDS, and, to gain his favor, organizations may decide to back AIDS whereas they may not otherwise have done so. Finally, although agencies do not receive staff, there is also no direct cost to them as AIDS is currently operating. The case coordinators' salaries are paid entirely by the county, or, if agencies pay them, they are reimbursed through Purchase of Care.

This project has been concerned primarily with *client coordination* and the development of *cooperation* between agencies. *Comprehensiveness,* although originally a concern in the SCS project, was largely lost in the AIDS project as the focus became case management. Indeed the two projects illustrate how much difference there is between an emphasis on filling all gaps in service (a problem of the comprehensiveness of programs) and an emphasis on having clients receive all available programs (a problem of the comprehensiveness of client care).

5

Government Agencies:
Los Angeles

The distinguishing characteristic of the Los Angeles project was the creation of a board of agencies—the Mental Retardation Services Board (MRSB)—rather than a board of individuals. This board was composed of twelve public agencies—state, county, and city—and one member who represented all private agencies associated with the Welfare Planning Council, a community-chest organization in the Los Angeles area. The MRSB centered its primary attention on planning and developing a delivery system for the mentally retarded in contrast to the Milwaukee and Bridgeport projects, which focused on the immediate situation of the clients themselves. The Los Angeles project was more similar in design and execution to the one in Cleveland, although there were still differences in approach since the board of the Cleveland project was composed to a great extent of prominent individuals in the community. There was also some similarity to the second phase (the AIDS project) in Milwaukee; however AIDS was a coalition of organizations with funds channeled through the department of public welfare, whereas in Los

Angeles funds were awarded to the board. Also the emphasis on public health and welfare agencies in Los Angeles contrasted sharply with the case in Milwaukee, where a number of private agencies were involved as partners.

The change strategy in this demonstration project was both innovative and extremely well thought out. The essential idea was that the traditional approaches to solving welfare problems—either the voluntary interest-group approach as in Bridgeport or the classic community-organization approach as in Cleveland—would not work because of fundamental changes in the political economy of the typical urban community. One such change was in sources of money, which were now large public bureaucracies (taxes) rather than private charities (donations). As a consequence, the power of prominent and wealthy industrialists had decreased, and the power of legislatures had increased. Consequently, administrators of public bureaucracies controlled large budgets, and they had become powerful and influential. Another change which affected the choice of strategy in this project was the continuous movement toward specialization, which meant that the casual good-willed person could no longer make as effective an imprint as before. With the growth in technology, a wide variety of expertise was necessary. Again, the result was not only to increase the importance of the professional or expert but also to put the emphasis on public bureaucracies, which had large staffs of experts.

Thus, the heart of the strategy was to bring together the major public agencies at the state, county, and city level in a contractual arrangement. The leaders of these organizations could then channel funds into the area of mental retardation. Since they were the major powers, they could affect legislation to get increased appropriations, and since they had many experts on their staffs, they could solve the technological problems inherent in a delivery system; more particularly they could develop the new programs required to fill in gaps in service. In this strategy the private sector was largely ignored.

A corollary of this strategy was that federal government funding would also be largely ignored. Unlike the other four demonstration grants, this one represented only a part of the total budget and was in existence for only three years. Further-more, it began after—albeit only a few months after—the MRSB had been created and funded from state and county sources. The staff and board members were specifically concerned about the desirability of relying upon federal funds, which were cor-rectly perceived as likely to be temporary. From the beginning, the leaders of the MRSB wanted to create a coordinating struc-ture which would have a reliable and permanent source of fund-ing, namely taxes from California and Los Angeles County.

Anyone who has visited Los Angeles knows how distinc-tive it is in comparison with most other metropolitan areas in the United States. In 1970, there were 7,039,075 people in the metropolitan area—more than double the population of the San Francisco metropolitan area and about five times that of either Milwaukee or Cleveland. Because of rapid growth and the desire of many people to own their own homes, the city and surround-ing satellite communities grew horizontally, spreading and sprawling over an unusually large area. The county is large enough to hold the cities of Denver, Chicago, St. Louis, Phila-delphia, New York, and Pittsburgh with space left over. Fur-thermore, by 1960 most of the county—with the exception of some mountains and oil wells—was part of a single metropolitan system. Because of the large area and number of people in-volved, many more organizations are needed to meet the needs of the populace than would be merited on a per capita basis. Organizations serving the mentally retarded are no exception. In the early 1960s, there were approximately 335 public and pri-vate agencies which in some way provided services for the men-tally retarded. About one third of these were school districts, indicating how fragmented and complex the mental retardation delivery system in Los Angeles County was—far more so than the systems in the other three large cities studied.

The major state agencies concerned with mental retarda-tion when the project started were the Employment Depart-ment, which is concerned with unemployment benefits and with various training programs for those who are difficult to employ; the Mental Hygiene Department, which provides most of the state funds for mental health on a matching basis with local communities; the Public Health Department, which is concerned mainly with community health programs; the Rehabilitation Department, which purchases services with federal and state funds for those who need rehabilitation; the Social Welfare Department, which does liaison work with local programs; the Education Department, which does liaison work with local programs. The major county agencies were the Health Department, which provides community health programs; the Mental Health Department, which does the same for mental health; Public Social Service, which provides all social-work services; and hospitals, which provide medical care. Beyond this there were two school systems: Los Angeles City, which has a department of special education; Los Angeles County, which includes many of the suburban school systems that have their own departments of special education.

A larger number of sheltered workshops, nursing homes, and other private agencies provided services for the mentally retarded. Unlike the situation in Milwaukee, however, no one particular workshop or other private agency stood out in the community except for Children's Hospital. It, however, became a critical actor when it, along with four other agencies including the University of Southern California Medical School, was designated as the site of the regional center, created by state legislation to be an area diagnostic-counseling-service center for services to the mentally retarded. The center in Los Angeles was one of the two set up on an experimental basis in the state in 1965. (The other was in San Francisco.) The regional-center concept was expanded to a statewide system by 1969 legislation.

Awareness Stage

Given this complexity, coordination of services for the mentally retarded in Los Angeles was a dominant theme. Like air pollution, the lack of coordination and the need for planning were easy to perceive in Los Angeles because the problems were so overwhelming and difficult.

Before coordination and planning could begin, it was important to gain the cooperation and support of various elites in the community. The organizers concentrated on two elites—highly placed organizational leaders and professional or technical experts—with greater emphasis on the experts. Task forces were formed with an overall steering committee consisting of the three original organizers—one from the State Mental Hygiene Department, the second from the Welfare Planning Council, and the third from the Department of Special Education of the Los Angeles City School system—plus several key members of the academic community. The head of the steering committee, not one of the three original organizers of the project, was chosen on the basis of his extensive contacts throughout the Los Angeles area. Then, a larger project committee was constituted. Most members of the project committee were technical experts who at the same time were, for the most part, quite highly placed within organizations and agencies in the area; they enjoyed positions of authority within their respective agencies if not necessarily power within the community. Thus, among others, there were several deans, the area directors of the appropriate state agencies, the directors of various private fund-raising agencies, and the directors of several city and county agencies or their assistants. This combination of expertise and organizational authority was probably a key factor in the later acceptance of the plan.

One begins to appreciate how different this elite was by comparing the names with those involved in the building of the Los Angeles Civic Center and the Museum of Art. In these major cultural efforts, the more traditional elite, the prominent, prestigeful, and wealthy families, was visible. The large size of Los Angeles County allows for differentiation of elites, with specialization in various community problems, such as mental retardation.

Shortly after the formation of the steering committee and the project committee, a series of subcommittees was established, centering around major areas: clinical services, educational services, rehabilitation and employment services, and social services. Thus, still more individuals were drawn into the initial stage of gaining support. All told, close to eighty people were involved.

These individuals were willing to lend their names to the project for several reasons. First, commitment at this stage was minimal; the goals at this point were simply to ascertain the needs of the mentally retarded and to determine gaps in services. Second, the President's Panel on Mental Retardation (1962) had called attention to the need for surveying services for the mentally retarded in the community. Third, the three original organizers were themselves well placed and together knew personally most of the persons asked to participate.

Although ostensibly the subcommittees were designed to develop proposals, in fact the bulk of the work was done by Ivy Mooring, who became project director of the MRSB, and her assistant, who patiently interviewed the heads and appropriate subordinates of many of the 335 agencies concerned with problems of mental retardation. The task forces and subcommittees gave legitimacy to Mooring when she made calls for interviews. This procedure grew out of a realistic appraisal of what was likely to emerge from the various subcommittees, the members of which had busy schedules and were volunteering their evenings. Mooring prepared careful proposals for the subcommittees, which, in turn, discussed, altered, and modified them. Many of those who participated found this to be a sound and effective procedure since most committees simply chase each member's bright proposal until it is dead with qualifications and a new one is made. Committees can work more effectively with agendas and written proposals that are well conceived and thought out. Qualifications by members then often lead to improvements in the document.

In addition to the cooperation of elites in the community, resources were also needed. The three individuals who started the project were each in a strategic position to provide some resources for Mooring and her staff. The member of the State Mental Hygiene Department was instrumental in gaining funds for the survey. The member of the Welfare Planning Council provided the physical location and neutral auspices. The member of the Department of Special Education in the Los Angeles City Schools suggested the appointment of Mooring, who had training in educational psychology, as coordinator of the project. The importance of Mooring's training and personality cannot be overstressed. With her qualifications (a Ph.D.) and her forceful personality, she was an ideal person for conducting a survey of needs and services. She was persistent and successful in gaining access to key individuals.

Her persistence and ability paid off handsomely in the final mental retardation survey (1963-1965), which reported on the situation and needs of the mentally retarded in Los Angeles County. Indeed, the mental retardation survey is a model of what can be done, given the right approach and organization. It included a brief and succinct discussion of the services that then existed, but, more important, it enumerated problems and difficulties, including missing services. Its most distinctive feature, however, was its first recommendation, which called for the creation of a board of public agencies as well as the creation of a welfare commission composed of private agencies which would have one representative on the board. Seldom do surveys make such a recommendation. More often reports are much vaguer, noting the need for greater coordination of existing services, the necessity to eliminate duplicated efforts, and the like. This survey was concrete and detailed, and it embodied specific ideas about what an effective service delivery system might look like.

Initiation Stage

The essential idea of the three individuals who started the project was that if coordination was to be effective, it would have to be among the big public agencies, both state and local, because they had and would continue to have most of the resources. Thus they got each of the twelve major public agencies to sign the joint-powers agreement, which simply stipulated that they agreed to agree. It did not contain any binding commitments beyond the willingness to meet together to discuss the creation of effective services for the mentally retarded. The agreement did give veto power to the head of the County Mental Health Department, which provided 25 percent matching funds under provisions of the California law on mental health (the Short-Doyle Act). The joint-powers agreement was signed also by the governor's office and the Los Angeles County Board of Supervisors.

Analysis of strategy. The members of the subcommittees played a critical role. By lending their names to the survey, they endorsed not only the findings but the recommendation for a board of public agencies as well. This endorsement served two critical purposes. First, high officials such as those in the governor's office and the Los Angeles County Board of Supervisors, hesitated to argue against so many technical experts and professionals in the county, especially well placed ones. Second, members of the subcommittees, depending upon their degree of commitment to the proposal, campaigned within their respective organizations for the proposal. In some instances, this campaigning was simple because the participant was the head of the agency. In most cases, however, the individual, at least for the major agencies, was at the second, third, or even fourth echelon within these large bureaucracies.

Most participants whom we interviewed placed great stress on the personality of Mooring as another factor in acceptance of the joint-powers agreement. She also had several key contacts on the Los Angeles County Board of Supervisors. In addition, the head of the County Mental Health Department threw his weight behind the proposal. He, too, knew various members of the Board of Supervisors.

Another factor that facilitated the signing of the joint-powers agreement was the availability of state funds on a matching basis. Because of the general wording of the Short-Doyle Act, the State Mental Hygiene Department could allocate money for mental retardation coordination efforts. The County Mental Health Department agreed to provide matching funds for several reasons. First, it thereby acquired veto power over the actions of the MRSB. Second, it would get considerable money for a small investment—the ratio at the time being 75 percent state and 25 percent city or county. Third, it gained participation in a service delivery area that was potentially an important one. Fourth, as a relatively highly professionalized and decentralized structure, it probably prided itself on its toleration and support of innovations (see Hage and Aiken, 1970, for evidence on this point). Thus, the nature of its budgeting as well as its goals encouraged the agency to enter a large number of cooperative efforts.

The use of federal monies for the MRSB was not conceived as part of the original plan. However, when the opportunity arose, federal monies could be used to supplement the state and county funding. The composition of the board opened channels of communication and thus facilitated obtaining information about the availability of federal funds. Just as the information about the possibility of obtaining Short-Doyle funds came from one of the state agencies that was to participate in the project, so the fact that the Vocational Rehabilitation Administration (VRA) was planning to fund several projects in coordination of services for the mentally retarded was called to the attention of Mooring by the representative from the state rehabilitation department. A grant request was prepared, and it was funded shortly after the MRSB came into existence.

Goals. The original objective of the MRSB was the development of coordinated services for the mentally retarded with major emphasis on filling in the many gaps and eliminating duplication. The survey delineated a large number of specific objectives, regarding programs and resources, consistent with this objective. Little attention was paid to the problem of client coordination. However, over time, the emphasis switched from coordination to planning, for reasons outlined below.

Implementation Stage

Structure. The MRSB was the brain-child largely of one man, who at the time was on the Welfare Planning Council and was one of the original three who organized the technical and organizational elites in the community to carry out the mental retardation survey. He reported to us that this model was based on an earlier effort in Los Angeles County, a youth opportunity board which had been established in the early sixties and had worked well.

Given the assumption that the future lay with the public

agencies, every state, city, and county agency even remotely connected with mental retardation was included in the original plan. This choice of members was a consequence not only of their large budgets. Each of the agencies handled large client populations and had extensive contact with the general population. Furthermore, their large staffs gave them weight in the community above and beyond their client constituency. From a practical point, these organizations and their staffs were making most of the decisions about the services to be provided, where they were to be provided, and who was to provide them, and thus they logically should have been represented on the board.

In addition to the board, with its representatives from each of the organizations that signed the joint-powers agreement, MRSB also had staff members at its disposal. Mooring became the project director, and various signatory agencies supplied staff from time to time.

The representatives of each of the organizations on the MRSB varied somewhat in their power within the organizations they represented. In addition, the amount of contact each agency had with the problem of retardation affected the nature of the involvement of the person who represented that organization. It also affected the selection of the president of the MRSB. Here a dilemma arose. Ideally the most powerful person in an agency should have been its representative. Then, if the MRSB agreed to develop a given policy, action could be taken relatively quickly and a new program or service begun. However, mental retardation was only one problem area for many of these agencies, and, over time, the board representative became the individual most concerned with the problem of mental retardation in a particular agency. Thus someone with diminished authority for committing the agency to action spoke for the agency at meetings of the MRSB. As this switch in the authority of representatives began to occur, the power of the MRSB began to diminish.

Planning. Like the mental retardation survey, which attempted to determine the nature of available services and to identify gaps in service, the planning study completed by Mooring and her staff was excellent. They studied the geographical distribution of the mentally retarded in the county and compared this distribution with the availability and distribution of services. The joint-powers agreement helped facilitate access to records of the agencies which signed it so that some nine thousand mentally retarded individuals (checked for duplications) were identified and located by city census block. The names of these individuals were obtained through the cooperation of all public school districts in the county, Public Social Service, hospitals, nurseries, resident facilities, and day-care centers. Not unexpectedly, the services available were generally not located where most of the mentally retarded were.

Considerable thought was given to how to develop and deliver services in the vast and amorphous sprawl of Los Angeles. Dividing the county into separate service areas was much more complicated than might appear on the surface. The goal was to create sufficiently large service areas so that economies of scale could be effected and so that the efficiency of the service delivery system would be maximized. But, the boundaries of these new service areas also had to be congruent with the boundaries of other service delivery systems. Therefore, an attempt was made to combine the mental retardation service areas with the comprehensive health planning areas, mental health regions, and public health districts, the boundaries of which were largely congruent. The size of the population in each service area was to be between 1,250,000 and 1,500,000, while the size of the estimated population of mentally retarded was to be between 25,000 and 29,000 in each area. Mooring developed and gave presentations explaining this concept, complete with charts, and these proved to be effective in winning support for proposals. In addition, the representatives of the various agencies on the MRSB increased the visibility of the need to coordinate the various service areas in a comprehensive plan. And the plan gained in sophistication because of the variety of problems of the agencies represented on the board.

Another strength of the Los Angeles plan was that gradually the concept of a comprehensive service delivery system for the mentally retarded emerged. While all five community projects recognized to some extent the need for a fixed point of referral and a continuum of care as outlined in the report of the President's Panel on Mental Retardation, the Los Angeles concept of a service delivery system was more comprehensive than most (see Mental Retardation Services Board, 1968). While it was never implemented because of difficulties that occurred with the creation of the new regional center, it does indicate the extent of the planning that occurred.

The final distinctive feature of the plan was its identification of areas of poverty as major concentrations of the mentally retarded. While some attention was paid to the problem of cultural definitions of mental retardation, the attempt to link incidence of mental retardation with potential causes, such as the cultural deprivation often implied by poverty, helped to underscore what might be involved in long-term solutions to the problem of mental retardation and also provided a strong argument for locating more services in the deprived neighborhoods of Los Angeles County.

Expansion of services. During its first two years, from 1965 to 1967, most meetings of the MRSB centered on implementing some of the recommendations of the mental retardation survey. A considerable amount of attention was paid to the Los Angeles City school system for several reasons. First, the experience of Mooring was in this area. As a former employee of the Department of Special Education, she was most familiar with this aspect of a delivery system for the mentally retarded. Second, one of the major gaps identified in the survey was in this area. And, third, some efforts in this direction had already been made.

At the same time, there was a major obstacle, namely the Los Angeles City school system. Even though a signatory to the joint-powers agreement, the city school system was not eager to allocate money to these services. The MRSB therefore organized among community agencies a campaign in which the information from the mental retardation survey was used to convince the city school system of the necessity of establishing classes for the trainable mentally retarded. Throughout the campaign the representative from the city school system on the MRSB was actively working to build support for this idea within his organization. While the campaign by the MRSB was probably decisive in the agreement of the city school system to expand the number of classrooms for the trainable mentally retarded, the invidious comparison with the Los Angeles County schools, which had taken far more initiative in this area, was also a factor.

The need for preschool programs for children ages three to five had also been identified as a key problem in the mental retardation survey. Members of the MRSB noted that existing legislation (the California Compensatory Education Act) might be a source of support for such a program. A ruling by state authorities was favorable, and the first center was established in 1966. The three agencies involved were all represented on the board—the State Social Welfare Department, the Department of Education, and the county Public Social Service. A great deal of coordination was attained through this program, and a person was assigned to the staff of the MRSB to act as coordinator.

Both these efforts illustrate MRSB success in obtaining financial resources. They also illustrate two different strategies. The first might be called freeing funds within an agency, that is, reallocation of existing resources to different priorities. Needless to say, this strategy is extremely difficult, and the city school system was the major place where the MRSB was able to effect this kind of action. Given the reluctance of the school system to become involved and the difficulty of getting an organization to change its priorities, it was an impressive victory.

The easier strategy, since it does not necessarily affect the internal structure and interests of an organization, is to locate new sources of funding. This strategy accounts for most of the effectiveness of the MRSB. Use of this second strategy involved little dependence on the MRSB board, but much on the staff and its knowledge about future sources of money.

The importance of the MRSB for obtaining money is also exemplified in its assistance to several agencies in the writing of research grants. For example, one was written to create home training services; and a hospital was also aided in its preparation of grant proposals.

Mobilizing community support. The importance of the MRSB for mobilizing community support is illustrated in the help it gave to a bill designed to fund developmental disabilities centers on a permanent basis. The MRSB gained signatures for the bill and threw its expertise and contacts into the legislative battle. However, it is hard to determine how decisive this support was. Some legislators with whom we talked felt that the bill would have been passed in any event.

Coordinating programs. Not much program coordination occurred, at least in the opinion of those who were involved. One problem, as perceived by persons whom we interviewed, was that the MRSB did not have power because of the absence of sanctions in the agreement. As long as the MRSB had no control over funding, it could not effect much change. Whatever was accomplished was done primarily with persuasion. Although this was the perception of the people involved in the project, it is not in our opinion accurate. The MRSB had much more power than did any of the other structures established in the demonstration projects. And although it had persuasion as a device, it was in a different position because of the joint-powers agreement. The inclusion of the Los Angeles City school system, the change in their policy, and the ability to change the policy of the regional center (see below) were striking achievements compared with those of the other projects. Furthermore, up to the passage of the Lanterman Act in 1969, the MRSB had a secure basis of funding.

The most interesting example of attempts to coordinate services involved the regional center. In 1965 the Waldie Act created regional diagnostic-counseling-service centers under the jurisdiction of the State Mental Hygiene Department on an experimental basis. The Lanterman Act of 1969 further extended this concept by creating a new community board, which made the MRSB obsolete. Los Angeles was awarded the contract for a center in 1965, but it went to a private organization, the Children's Hospital, which had been campaigning for the legislation and which had a long history of involvement in the mental retardation field. The MRSB, with its inadequate representation of private agencies, was at a serious disadvantage. The

MRSB could not reconstitute itself to include such agencies because this would require a new joint-powers agreement. Neither could it supervise or exercise control over the regional center. Thus, a key element in the comprehensive service delivery system for the mentally retarded was, in effect, not part of the MRSB.

The board and Mooring tried in various ways to help bring about changes in the operation of the regional center from 1965 to 1969. Much of the money allocated to the regional center was spent at the hospital itself at first, mainly on residential care. This policy created some dissatisfaction on the part of MRSB members, but they could do little about it. The MRSB did hold a series of meetings designed to change the policy of the regional center and to emphasize its concern with delivery of services. Through these meetings, the MRSB was able to effect some changes in the policies of the regional center, specifically toward less institutional care and more attempts to become a fixed point of referral.

The MRSB had considerable success in gaining cooperation among professionals in the various agencies. Almost everyone perceived that cooperation as a positive contribution of the MRSB, and almost all mentioned this consequence spontaneously. One method for attaining cooperation was through placement of staff on a loan basis in the central headquarters. This proved to be an effective mechanism, in addition to the MRSB meetings, for creating communications channels among agencies.

The MRSB accomplished about as much as did most of the other projects in developing comprehensiveness through several new programs. And, like the others, the MRSB accomplished little in the area of compatibility among programs, in part because little attention was paid to client coordination. Although one joint program was developed, it was the significant exception.

Analysis of Strategy

Displacement of goals. As the MRSB was less and less successful in implementing services or expanding existing ones, it moved more and more to a preoccupation with planning, a

visible product. The ability to coordinate and implement programs depended to a great extent on new funding becoming
available; in most cases, reallocating existing funds, often locked
into concrete obligations and tight budgets, proved to be impossible. The VRA grant allowed the staff to do the planning
study, and, not unexpectedly, as more staff became involved in
this activity, it evolved into a major goal of the project.

Even the planning objectives became subverted in the last
year of the VRA grant as the MRSB had to struggle with both
the blacks and the browns who wanted membership on the
board. Since the MRSB was composed of agencies, there was no
way of allowing them without writing a new contract. But
minority groups felt that this excuse was simply an attempt to
prevent them from having access to power. This conflict
occurred in a city with one of the lowest percentages of black
population. But it was also the city where the first major black
riot—Watts—occurred during the 1960s. And it was a city in
which the black community had made a good deal of progress
in other areas. As a consequence, aspirations of black people
were high, and minority groups were attempting to reach centers of power. The MRSB had high visibility in the community,
it appeared to be a power center, and therefore it was approached. Minority leaders did not realize that the MRSB did
not have much power or money, most of which were in the
separate agencies represented on the MRSB. The many meetings
generated by this issue absorbed much of the energy of the
MRSB for more than a year and deflected it from further
attempts at coordination or planning. There was the additional
complication that the Lanterman Act of 1969 required the
establishment of boards for the regional centers that represented the community. Thus, the problem was to solve both
issues and at the same time preserve the joint-powers agreement.
Understandably, goals became subverted and displaced over the
issue of survival.

Organizational autonomy, even with a joint-powers agreement, was another factor that probably contributed to the
desire to do planning. It was a political necessity to avoid direct
competition with any of the signatory agencies. In addition,

there was the specific policy of not having the staff of the MRSB become involved in direct service. Then, too, planning was an important need given the urban sprawl of Los Angeles. Thus, the shift in goals was inevitable given the nature of the board and the various funding restrictions placed upon it.

Factors affecting implementation of services. Almost all those interviewed felt that the MRSB was not effective in developing innovative programming. Likewise, little cooperative programming occurred as a consequence of MRSB leadership. The innovative programming that did occur, and there were several examples, especially in community organization, often resulted when staff personnel were loaned from one agency to another. Under such circumstances, staff members could see problems from the vantage point of the larger community and were likely to recognize new needs as well as solutions to them. But, the source of such innovations was the delivery side—that is, the ideas were generated by the staff, not by members of the board.

One of the greatest strengths of the board and this kind of change strategy was in its ability to muster support, gain funds, and affect legislation. Perhaps the best achievement of the MRSB in the eyes of its members was the passage of the Lanterman Act, which increased the number of regional centers and established area boards composed of professionals, parents, and other community interests to do planning and coordination. But despite all the activity of the MRSB in getting this legislation passed, and there was a great deal (including telephone calls to party leaders), it is hard to assess fully its impact. Members of the San Francisco project also claimed to have had a major hand in this achievement. Few state officials involved in this legislation believed that either the San Francisco or the Los Angeles project had much influence and that the legislation would have been passed without their agitation. The truth of the matter undoubtedly lies somewhere between these two extremes.

The difficulty of assessing the specific impact of the MRSB in this one, but critical, area is surpassed by the difficulty of determining the overall influence of the MRSB on the situation of the mentally retarded in Los Angeles County. Many of the individuals interviewed believed that the lot of the mentally retarded would have been improved even without the existence of the MRSB; the city schools would have gradually added more classrooms, agencies would have found out about and obtained grants, the Lanterman Act would have been passed, and so on. But a sizable proportion felt that the MRSB made these things occur much faster than they might otherwise have occurred, probably an accurate assessment. The MRSB facilitated increasing awareness of the problems of the mentally retarded and the development of action programs on their behalf. It provided a structure that increased channels of communication between interested parties and brought about cooperation among the public agencies. Funds flowed rapidly into the community, and agencies moved to develop and expand services, even if overall there was not much innovative programming.

In attempting to assess the strengths and weaknesses of particular structures such as the MRSB, it is difficult to know how important particular personalities were relative to other factors. In this instance, the personality of Mooring looms large. She was disliked by some and praised by others, but everyone credited her with being an important factor in the successes of the MRSB. Members of any board lose sight of how dependent they are on full-time staff. A staff member who is able to think about problems for forty hours a week is in a position different from that of board members, whose commitments to such problems are obviously restricted (Harrison, 1959).

Routinization Stage

Perhaps one of the greatest weaknesses of the MRSB was its inability to change its structure and incorporate new leaders, such as representatives of parents groups, community groups, and minority groups. The problem of representation was largely resolved with the passage of the Lanterman Act, which called for community representation on area boards. The creation of these new area boards meant the demise of the MRSB, which voted itself out of existence in June 1970 and was replaced shortly afterward by the Mental Retardation Program Board-Area 10.

The MRSB probably would have survived if the Lanterman Act had not been passed. Unlike the projects in other communities, with the possible exception of the AIDS project in Milwaukee, the project in Los Angeles had solved its funding problem and had a secure financial base. Its demise was a consequence of the creation of the new board, which was designed to do much less, but perhaps make some interests in the community much happier in the process. Ironically, in lobbying in behalf of the Lanterman Act, the MRSB was instrumental in bringing about its own demise.

In this project we see *coordination at the resource and program level* with particular emphasis on resources. *Client coordination* was not considered and as a consequence certain problems were probably undetected. The structure of the MRSB was effective in creating much more *cooperation* among autonomous agencies but not among representatives of the clients and the agencies themselves.

6

Traditional Welfare Federation: Cleveland

In Cleveland, the Vocational Rehabilitation Administration (VRA) grant was given to the Welfare Federation, a large, prestigious, private federation of health and welfare agencies. Almost totally supported by the local United Appeal, this agency had a large staff of experienced professionals, primarily social workers, who made extensive use of classic community-organization methods to improve health and welfare services in the community. The grant itself was administered by a special mental retardation project of the Welfare Federation housed in downtown Cleveland.

Cleveland is a large industrial city situated in northeast Ohio at the mouth of the Cuyahoga River. Located at a meeting point of Lake Superior iron ore, Appalachian coal, and cheap immigrant labor, it has long been a major manufacturing center. Today it has many of the problems of American cities in general and in the eastern and industrial North in particular. The population of the city proper has been declining (14.3 percent decline between 1960 and 1970) and was less than one half the county population in 1970; at the same time the suburbs have been growing and thriving. Cuyahoga County, which includes Cleveland, grew 5 percent between 1960 and 1970.

Socioeconomic and demographic characteristics are typical of large industrial cities. Cleveland is 39 percent nonwhite. It has an ethnically diverse population, a large blue-collar working class, and ethnic, cultural, and economic diversity in the suburbs. However, observers usually see a somewhat greater private-regarding ethic than the average. Ethnic and neighborhood loyalties are fierce; social services are decentralized; and private efforts play a large role.

In many ways, the social and political climate in Cleveland has simply paralleled the national climate, particularly during the sixties: public expenditures, renewal, community awakening in the early sixties; disruption, riots, and radicalism in the middle and late sixties, along with the election of the first black mayor; recession, entrenchment, and conservatism as the seventies began, replete with the election of the first Republican mayor in several decades.

As in each of the other cities studied, a number of agencies besides the Welfare Federation were involved with the problem of mental retardation. A brief roster of some of the important agencies in this drama follows. The first seven existed at the beginning of the development project, while the two local boards, created by state legislation, came into being in 1967.

The Welfare Federation, with representatives from over 220 local health and welfare agencies, a professional staff of over thirty, and a successful history dating back to 1914, provided the auspices and physical location for the VRA grant. The project staff and committee could draw on the experience, prestige, and office facilities of the federation. Its close ties with the local United Appeal provided it with legitimacy and, more important, a secure source of funds.

The Parents-Volunteers Association originally was a local affiliate of a nationwide system of volunteer associations of parents of retarded children in state residential facilities. In Cleveland, this group became independent; it was large (over a thousand members) and powerful (raised over sixty thousand dollars per year).

The Council for the Retarded Child, the first private interest group for the retarded, had worked as early as the 1930s to pass legislation, improve services, and centralize private efforts.

The Cuyahoga County Association for Retarded Children was a parents-only group which broke away from the Council for the Retarded Child to centralize private volunteer efforts. A confederation of parent-run groups providing direct services (mainly training classes for the moderately to severely retarded), it had an agency membership of twenty-four and an individual membership of over one thousand. This group received funding and unofficial sanction from major agencies as the spokesman for parent interests.

The Bureau of Vocational Rehabilitation (BVR) was organized at the state level to administer federal vocational rehabilitation funds. Operating through a five-county regional office, with a regional staff of over 125, this group was the major purchaser of rehabilitation services for the educable retarded, servicing over one thousand retarded in 1970, about 10 percent of its total clients.

The Vocational Guidance and Rehabilitation Service (VGRS), a large (130 professional staff), private rehabilitation agency, shared a major facility on the east side of Cleveland with several other welfare and rehabilitation agencies.

The State Department of Mental Hygiene and Correction until 1968 included the Bureau of Mental Retardation, which was part of its Division of Mental Hygiene. At that time Mental Retardation was made a division of this department. It played a major role in the community through its administrative responsibilities and in framing the legislation which set up a planning and a service board in each county.

The Community Mental Health and Retardation Board (648 Board), a planning and service purchasing board, was set up by state legislation in 1967. It had a relatively small staff, but a secure source of funding for its large budget (three million dollars in 1970).

The County Board of Mental Retardation (169 Board), a

companion board to the 648, provided direct services (mainly education) to the retarded. It also had secure sources of funds and a large staff (two hundred professionals). It provided womb-to-tomb services for the retarded and took over many of the private classes and workshops which were active in early organizing efforts.

In addition, there existed the usual range of public and private agencies providing mainly generic services to the retarded, parallel to those we have seen in the other four demonstration projects.

Awareness Stage

Services for the retarded were increasing both in the state and in the Cleveland area in the late 1950s. Training classes, recreational facilities, and sheltered workshops were being started under private, usually parent, auspices, and these groups were instrumental in lobbying for legislation. Many of them were affiliated either with the Parents-Volunteers Association or with the Council for the Retarded Child. In 1959, however, the parents committee of the Council for the Retarded Child broke away from the main group claiming it did not have sufficient power in decision making. In late 1959, a parents-only organization, the Cuyahoga County Association for Retarded Children, was formed with the express intention of coordinating service and lobbying efforts. At about this time, private services for the retarded increased their demands on business and foundation sources of funds. Many groups began to sense a need for increased coordination among the already-existing service facilities. The Cleveland Growth Board (equivalent to the Chamber of Commerce), the Cleveland Foundation, the Parents-Volunteers Association, and the Council for the Retarded Child all suggested that the Welfare Federation provide leadership in this area.

Initiation Stage

With these rumblings of discontent, the Children's Council of the federation in 1960 began a small study of facilities for retarded children. A report of this committee to the federation board, approved in February 1963, recommended that additional staff activities be undertaken in behalf of mentally retarded adults as well as children. R. O. Buckman (a Ph.D. sociologist with a background in social work and community organization) was assigned three fourths time as a process analyst in the federation Health Goals Project and one fourth time in retardation in March 1963.

At a meeting held with VRA representatives in April 1963, Buckman was asked whether the federation would like to sponsor a demonstration project. Rehabilitation professionals assumed that the federation would be the logical auspices for such a project in Cleveland. Buckman indicated the federation would be interested, but that a planning phase would be necessary first to determine needs, to establish priorities, and to involve people who would support later implementation efforts. The compromise eventually agreed upon was that the VRA would fund both a planning phase and, if the need remained, a development phase. Approval for the planning phase was received in October 1964. By this time, a Mental Retardation Committee of about twenty-five professionals and parents had been operating for six months under the auspices of the Welfare Federation. The project mushroomed under the VRA grant; approximately $125,000 a year was budgeted between December 1965 and August 1971. During this period, services specifically for the retarded in the Cleveland area roughly tripled in size. This increase, however, paralleled a similar increase in public and private programs at the state level.

To a great extent, the mental retardation project was consciously designed by Buckman and other staff members according to tested community-organization principles and the experiences of the Welfare Federation. The whole project fell into four phases, only one of which was the VRA five-year grant period. In the preproject phase (March 1963 to October 1964) Buckman began exploring the local scene and building a staff and committee to be used to gain further resources for the retarded. The planning phase (October 1964 to December 1965) involved using a one-year $23,000 grant to develop a major planning document for the Cleveland area. Staff and committee involvement increased tremendously. During the development phase (December 1965 to December 1970) the committee and staff, expanded by the $125,000 VRA grant, implemented the recommendations of the planning document through community-organization techniques and some demonstration services. In the postproject phase (January 1971 through December 1971) Buckman departed, and most project activities were discontinued. The mental retardation field then operated under its own momentum.

Goals. The expectations of the VRA, the structure and capabilities of the Welfare Federation, the predilections of the staff (in particular those of Buckman), and prior statements of goals (such as those of the President's Panel on Mental Retardation, 1962) all influenced both the substantive goals and the means or methods (process goals) of the project. Many elements and factions in the community contributed to formulating a statement of goals and objectives based on research into community needs. Approved by the Mental Retardation Committee and the Welfare Federation board, this document (Greater Cleveland Mental Retardation Planning Project, 1965) contained sixty-two substantive and organizational recommendations which were to guide implementation during the development phase.

This and other documents published by the project suggest that the project staff was guided by the organizing principles and values of the classic community-organization approach. Dunham (1970, pp. 225ff.) points out several typical values held by community-organization theorists and practitioners: participation, consensus, use of professionals, cooperation, voluntary compliance rather than coercion, use of existing generic services, voluntary agencies paralleling government bureaus, and confederation rather than total merger.

Conscious adherence to community-organization principles is noted by Buckman in her final report (1971c). The Welfare Federation had used these techniques for years. Using a private agency as a base from which to initiate self-help and coordination efforts fits in quite well with the relatively low profile of the laissez-faire government typical at the state and community level in Ohio, and the tradition of fragmentation of private efforts.

Strategy. The project had five distinctive organizing guidelines: information, communication, and persuasion were the keys to implementation, rather than governmental authority or direct provision of services; professional central staff members were to act as researchers and organizing catalysts; a central policy-making committee was to be made up of volunteers; resources and initiative were to be decentralized rather than centrally controlled; and the project structure was to be a temporary stimulus, which when removed would leave behind services and organizations that could then continue to develop on their own.

Because the project did not have the authority or funds to centralize power or resources in order to achieve efficient coordination, the project set off to centralize information, which included doing research, producing documents, and establishing communication. The assumption was that awareness of a common goal and of the actions of others in achieving this goal would lead agencies to voluntarily change their behavior. When harmony was not brought about by simple information sharing, the project used influential people in the community and extensive research and expertise to persuade individuals and agencies to comply with the general directions of the plan. Only rarely did the project take a definite public stand on a specific issue and make a total commitment to either implement or block it.

As part of the information-sharing process, the project put out various documents: factual information about needs and resources, handbooks on how to set up or operate various services, and statements of policy and specific objectives. The first two could be produced simply by having competent technical staff members perform the necessary research and then write them. Because the policy statements required wide participation, a committee structure, made up of representatives of the retardation community, was established.

The Welfare Federation in Cleveland had long tried to involve citizens in every level of operations, and thus there was a clear precedent for the mental retardation project committee structure. This structure had three functions: to improve the quality of information by involving those with technical expertise, to improve the representativeness of policy by seeking opinions of relevant actors, and to secure compliance by increasing the commitment of participants to project goals. The Mental Retardation Committee was an ongoing discussion and policy-making group of important persons representing various segments of the community. It met once a month to discuss and pass resolutions on retardation issues. The subcommittees of the main committee involved other influential people and technical experts to research particular issues for reference back to the main committee.

Given that the project did not have either legal authority or large financial resources, Buckman felt it unrealistic to expect to create either a central joint-powers coordinating agency or a single superagency which would deliver all needed services. Therefore, the project encouraged decentralization of both initiative and resources. Organizations were not asked to change particular programs or perform specific services. Thus a large mosaic of services was to be provided in different ways by diverse agencies. Coordination would come to some extent through standardization of procedures but mostly through participation on an information-sharing committee.

Finally, the project was to be only a temporary stimulus. It must, therefore, be evaluated not only by its accomplishments during operation, but also by the structure it left behind. A procedure can be adequate while being applied, but have no lasting effect once removed.

Implementation Stage

Structure. The Welfare Federation provided both funds and a prestige base through its affiliation with United Appeal, which was a fund-collection agency with ultimate control over Welfare Federation policies through power of the purse. United Appeal, the Welfare Federation, the Community Planning Division of the federation, and the mental retardation project all had policy-making boards made up of professionals and influential people in the community. While this connection with the community power structure put constraints on how radical federation activities could be, it also provided the federation with ready support for project activities. The federation staff was experienced and stable, but the structure was also flexible enough to allow addition of the mental retardation project with its needs for a degree of autonomy and discretion.

The project staff was experienced. Most had master's degrees in social work, and many had experience in community-organization activities. Except for Buckman, who kept her position throughout the project, there were two separate staffs, one for the planning phase and one for the development phase. The staff turnover was rather low, probably because of the experience and size of the federation: knowledgeable staff members were recruited, they found the working conditions suitable, and the federation provided opportunities for future careers after the project ended. The flexibility and participatory nature of the project increased morale.

While the full-time professional staff members were formally subordinate to the citizen committees, they had the predominant influence over policy and operations. Dual-authority problems of the sort that surfaced in the Bridgeport project did not occur here. As one respondent put it, "We were all polite to each other." The methods and means of the project were largely prestructured both by the staff (in particular, Buckman) and by federation tradition. To a great extent, the role of committee members was predetermined; there was little to do but conform to this approach or resign. For whatever reason, many committee members simply participated little or did resign. One member commented that the staff could have written all the reports themselves with the same content, but would not have gotten the support they did without involving the committee. Most committee members did not feel they were being manipulated, though they were conscious that there was a strong director. There was also a high degree of mutual influence. But with the staff members' status as employees of the agency which contracted for the grant (they were not hired by the committee as were staff members in San Francisco and Bridgeport) and with their experience and competence in retardation, they were able to structure and channel committee efforts in a fairly united direction.

Committee members were originally selected by Welfare Federation staff (Buckman and her supervisors) in conjunction with the first chairman of the committee. Replacements were nominated by a committee selected by Buckman. Members had to be formally approved by the Community Planning Division board, but this approval usually amounted to rubber-stamping. While there was an attempt to include representatives from all segments and factions of the retardation field, there was also great caution at first to select persons who could work together. Almost the whole first year was devoted to experimenting with different combinations of members. After that, there was relatively little turnover (only seventy-four persons altogether for thirty positions in seven years), and much of the turnover was among those who participated little.

We can categorize the individuals who were on the committee into four groups: parents of retarded, influential people in the community (persons selected for their influence or competence in some area unrelated to retardation, such as bankers, lawyers), retardation professionals (both independent professionals—a large number of medical doctors—and agency heads), and multiple volunteers (persons who were not parents of retardates but who had multiple ties to volunteer social-service organizations). Thus, links with both the community power structure and the major mental retardation agencies were provided. Of the seventy-four committee members, 15 percent were parents of retarded; 21 percent, influential people in the community; 39 percent, professionals; and 25 percent, multiple volunteers. Thus, professionals were represented most heavily, although members were not chosen primarily because of their professional ties and were not meant to formally represent agencies they belonged to. Almost all members were of high socioeconomic status.

The Mental Retardation Committee consisted of twenty-four to thirty people influential in retardation. During the development phase, it held two-hour monthly meetings. It was supplemented with subcommittees and task forces when necessary, which drew in additional persons. The committee membership and size and the degree of community involvement and commitment of members were all important variables carefully monitored by the project staff.

Because many divergent views were represented on the committee, it did not attempt major projects for which a great deal of consensus would be required and in which success or failure would be immediately evident. The purpose of the committee was primarily to produce policy statements. Thus, it spent a major portion of its time in resolving differences. Further unity of purpose was provided by the fact that committee participation varied tremendously. Several individuals spent a large amount of time on committee activities, and influence gravitated toward them.

Throughout the project, subcommittees existed, at least on paper, for each of five major functional areas: vocational training, recreation, residential facilities, clinical facilities, and education. Subcommittees were composed of main committee members (each belonged to one subcommittee) and outside experts. Almost one hundred persons participated.

The major additional committee was the Blueprint Task Force, formed in 1965 to research needs and compose a planning document which would be the working guide of the development phase. The task force had some Mental Retardation Committee members and involved seventy-five persons altogether. The task force was also organized into subcommittees, each responsible for a particular service area.

The major arena for participation of agency heads was the Agency Forum, which met an average of three times per year for conferences on special topics. All agency heads were invited, and conferences were open to any interested party. No policy decisions were made; the forum was reserved primarily for communication among professionals on technical matters. It thus provided participation for professionals without encumbering the committee with too large or too reluctant a membership.

Information services. The project staff and committees did considerable research on Cleveland area services. Much of this information was published in various state and regional plans and in documents put out by the project. Two major reports were the "Guide to Services for the Mentally Retarded: Greater Cleveland Area," which was a listing of agencies providing services and which went through five editions, and the "Directory of Services," which was an annotated guide for use by professionals and which went through two editions. A large fact book, giving further details about retardation, was compiled, and about one hundred copies were distributed. In addition, several handbooks on how to operate direct services were prepared.

The need for information and referral services became apparent as numerous requests for information about services were received. In 1966 a project staff person was added to the Community Information Service (CIS), already in operation in the federation. The CIS was simply a centralized source of information about social services with counseling limited to advice on which ones were most appropriate for the situation. In 1969, the retardation component was augmented with the assignment of two additional staff members. These assistants expanded their efforts to include a minimal amount of case management—following a client through for perhaps a dozen phone calls or attending a case conference over several days. During 1969, the most active year, 1,354 separate inquiries were received, and 2,101 calls and other contacts were used in responding to them. These information and referral specialists were directly paid by project funds, though they operated within the CIS division of the Welfare Federation, and they were located in the same building as the project. One information and referral staff position was continued after the project ended. In addition, during the project the information and referral staff began a pilot subproject to study the typical experiences of young retarded adults with rehabilitation services in the inner city. The project hoped to expand this study into another development project for the inner-city retarded. A grant application was submitted after the project ended but was not funded, and since no other local sources of funding were available, this project was not implemented.

Community organization. During the development phase, the Mental Retardation Committee and staff were involved largely in community organization. Their efforts to implement the sixty-two recommendations amounted to a continuation of the research and policy discussion started in the planning phase, but they added organizing efforts in the mental retardation community itself: offering consultation, participating in campaigns for bond levies, trying to get agency heads to work together, and the like. There was no central substantive goal, but rather a commitment to act as the organizing catalyst for a variety of efforts. The overall emphasis, however, changed somewhat. In the first three years the emphasis was primarily on the moderately to severely retarded, where the need was most visible and where support from parents groups was great. In the last two years, education and vocational rehabilitation were emphasized. To give an idea of how the project functioned, we have selected three important examples of organizing efforts that involved project staff.

Among the first efforts of the project staff was the provision of assistance to struggling sheltered workshops. The earliest target was Circle Workshop, a private, parent-run workshop for about sixty retarded in the downtown area. Sale of its products covered less than half its operating needs, and it had been having financial difficulties since it was founded in 1955. The project staff gave advice and consultation and even recommended to the Welfare Federation that a grant be given to the workshop, although the federation central planning board turned this request down. The staff did, however, arrange meetings with the VGRS, a multiservice rehabilitation agency supported partly by the United Appeal. Eventually Circle Workshop moved into the new VGRS center. Several other agencies occupied the same premises, including Goodwill Industries, United Cerebral Palsy, and the BVR. Although direct financial assistance was not provided to Circle Workshop, the physical proximity of several rehabilitation agencies afforded possibilities for increased interaction and coordination.

Closely related to this subproject was the first major attempt at provision of direct service on a demonstration basis, with the hope that local agencies would take over support for the service. This subproject was the wholly-funded Mobile Analysis and Rehabilitation Team (MART), whose purpose was to provide central staff support for seven workshops in a three-county area. There was little overlap in the services rendered by these workshops, partly because they were geographically distant. The MART program intended only to bring about a pooling of resources and to provide a common staff in order to achieve advantages of staff specialization, scale, and perhaps standardization. The project attempted to stimulate confederation by first sponsoring and underwriting the service, and then gradually decreasing its share of matching funds.

The MART did deliver many services, including efficient work and accounting procedures, 155 medical examinations, many individual counseling interviews, and intake and record-keeping methods.

The funding method used however militated against confederation. Sponsorship was not given to any one workshop so as to avoid the conflict in roles this would imply. The funds were not, however, given to a coalition of agencies, a committee made up of official representatives of workshops. Rather, VGRS, specialists in rehabilitation training, was simply funded to provide the service and distribute it to the participating workshops. The advisory board for the project did not even include representatives from all the workshops. At the prospect of having to put up their own money, which was in short supply, workshops balked at committing individual resources for a common effort. VGRS did not develop mechanisms to encourage such merger because it was in its interest to have the service remain outside the agencies; VGRS benefited by being the paid consultant. Thus neither VGRS nor any of the workshops found it in their interest to give up some autonomy and incur some costs to provide this joint program, even if it was needed. More important, the funding structure (direct payment to VGRS) did not require such cooperation. As a result this joint program ended when the project discontinued MART funding.

Efforts for the educable retarded were concentrated in the latter part of the development phase and were located in the vocational goals subcommittee, which had one staff member assigned to it from 1967 on—a young professional with a master's degree in public health who had been hired by the project the previous year. The educable retarded (IQ 50 to 75) in the Cleveland area had few programs for them except for special education programs in the schools, which tended to be dumping grounds for intractable students. Parents of educable retardates were not as effective in obtaining good programs as were parents of trainable retardates because they were often of lower socioeconomic status. In addition, black and other minority groups did not want to stress retardation as an issue of relative IQ, but rather as another symptom of systematic racial and class oppression.

The educable retarded have their best chance of gainful employment in manual jobs, but most vocational education programs in Cleveland had IQ standards which disqualified the educables. Experimental work-study programs for educable mentally retardates made no use of existing work-study facilities. The BVR, which was empowered to work with the educable retarded, did not itself provide training, evaluation, or sheltered work, but had to contract with other agencies for these. Further, the BVR had no joint programs with the schools.

The vocational goals staff person set out to improve coordination and joint programming, but had no organized client interest groups to work with. In addition, he was often working with large, bureaucratic structures and thus presumably ones resistant to joint programming (Aiken and Hage, 1968). Procedures were consistent with the project methods outlined above. Persons were contacted and consulted with, meetings were held, study trips were arranged, and eventually from all this research a model for the collaboration of vocational education, special education, and the BVR was developed. Based on conventional practice and the recommendation of professionals in the field, this flow chart prescribed a course for the individual high school-age retardate through these various agencies.

The staff member also worked closely with the Cuyahoga

East Program for Special Education, a new federation of four-teen suburban school districts formed by interested parents and professionals to apply for a federal Title VI staffing grant in developmental disabilities. It had a central staff located in the school which provided services for students in the member districts. No funds were committed by the individual school districts. The vocational goals staff person provided advice to this program and was named to its governing board. After withdrawal of federal funding in 1971, although the coordinating structure formally remained, the degree of cooperation receded. Few resources were voluntarily committed by any of the school districts to a central program; they were apparently waiting for new federal funding to pick up the tab for a central staff.

The vocational goals subproject shows clearly what can be expected when grass-roots community-organization principles of persuasion and voluntary cooperation are applied to large, public bureaucracies. Little effect can be attributed directly to the subproject because this work meshed with other efforts at the community, state, and federal levels. The subproject achieved some interagency communication and some loose forms of confederation, such as an association for work-study counselors. But no continuing large-scale joint programming or other coordinating structure was established.

Creation of two local boards. Two pieces of state legislation passed in 1967 profoundly affected the delivery system in Cuyahoga County. These were HB 648, which set up a community planning and funding structure, and SB 169, which set up a service delivery board in each county. The project staff had an important role in the design and passage of this legislation, but probably not a determining role since these bills were the product of political processes and forces operating to a great extent at the state and federal levels.

Because federal legislation required that a state and local planning structure be established in order to receive federal funds, a state planning structure for mental retardation was established in 1963. At first, it was just a component of the Mental Health Citizens Committees, which were operating at the state and local level. Then, a full-time staff position for retardation was funded at the state level. No money was given for such positions at the local level, but in the Cleveland region the Mental Retardation Committee and project staff acted as the citizen's committee and staff components. The sixty-two recommendations were submitted as the regional report of this committee and were incorporated in the state plan.

At the end of the federal grant period, the mental retardation staff at the state level was incorporated by the director of the Department of Mental Hygiene and Correction into the Mental Retardation Division. However, a structure was needed at the local level for retardation and mental health, both of which were part of the Department of Mental Hygiene and Correction. The director began working, then, on a bill which would provide this structure, preferably integrating mental health and mental retardation into one board. Such a structure would also extend bureaucratic control from the department to the local level. However, the legislature was wary of committing the state to additional expenditures. Similar bills had been proposed to the legislature several times before and had failed.

Several other grass-roots groups were pressing for similar legislation, though their interests were often in conflict. Both mental health associations in the state and the Ohio Association for Retarded Children (OARC) wanted legislation requiring that local governments provide programs for their clients. The retardation group, with a professional staff at the state level and therefore a significant lobbying force, did not want retardation services to be included in the same agency with mental health since they feared dominance by the latter. Thus while they were willing to have both types of services included in the same legislation, they wanted separate retardation services at the local level.

At the same time, local interests were concerned that local autonomy be preserved. On the second day of the legislative hearings, an informal committee of four prominent persons representing local interests appeared at the office of the director of the Department of Mental Hygiene and Correction and said that if local autonomy were not preserved, they would withdraw support from the legislation.

The project and committee were outside many of these conflicts, but they did strongly support the provision of services at the community level. Both Buckman and the committee chairman kept in touch weekly with the head of OARC and testified at the hearings, as they did on some of the other major hearings affecting the retarded. In February 1966, Buckman was invited to join the Joint Committee on Legislation and was subsequently named secretary. Buckman and other members of the committee made many inputs into the design of this legislation until it was signed by the governor in July 1967. It is difficult to unravel the exact amount and direction of project influence. A large mental retardation project from the largest city in the state would naturally have participated in such legislation. But most respondents seem to agree that the project was only one of several influences, that the project did not initiate the legislation, and that significant, perhaps sufficient, support existed independently of the project.

The resulting two bills show the strains of these conflicting forces. Bill 648 sets up a Community Mental Health and Retardation Board with a counterpart at the state level. It is primarily a planning, funding, and coordinating board with limited service delivery functions, including the temporary filling of gaps in services. For instance, in Cuyahoga County it cosponsors the information and referral service operated by the Cuyahoga County Association for Retarded Children. In Cuyahoga County the 648 Board consists of a staff of about ten persons, governed by a board of twelve (the law states from nine to fifteen). Two of the board members must be physicians, one third are appointed by the director of the Department of Mental Hygiene and Correction, and the rest by county commissioners; 75 percent of operating funds come from the state.

The 169 Board is the service delivery board. Its responsibility is stated somewhat vaguely as the administration of "programs in the county for the training of mentally retarded children and adults." In Cuyahoga County it took over county training classes for the retarded with IQs under 50, which amounted to about forty-five classes, and it took over most sheltered workshops. In July 1970, the bill was revised to bring residential centers under 169 jurisdiction and also to put the newly constructed comprehensive training centers directly under the State Division of Mental Retardation. Each local 169 Board has seven members, all of whom must be county residents and one of whom must be a parent of a retarded; all are appointed by local authorities. Funds to operate this program come from school districts in which the retardate would be a student if his intelligence were normal, from a state matching fund which supplies $450 per student, and from county funds such as special levies which can be put on the county ballot. A three-mill levy was passed in 1968 in Cuyahoga for construction funds.

The formal authority and the funding power of these two boards are greater than those of the mental retardation project. Both the 169 and 648 staffs have worked cooperatively with the project, and in conjunction with the Cuyahoga County Association for Retarded Children they have provided what Buckman calls a "four-legged stool" on which to base community planning and coordination. When these boards first went into operation, they relied on the accumulated experience of the project. Three persons the project recommended were placed on the 648 Board; and two persons on the 169 Board were committee members and heads of important agencies in retardation. The director of the 169 program was also recommended by the project staff, and the director of the 648 program is a former Welfare Federation staff member. Thus a great deal of mutual acquaintanceship and consensus exist among the heads of the four main agencies. Further, the first mental retardation plan which the 648 Board submitted to the state was essentially written by the project. The preparation and publicity for the first construction levy was done by the project. And the 648 Board did not have a specialized retardation planner until after the departure of Buckman, apparently because the project filled this role.

Analysis of Strategy

Displacement of goals. The classic treatments of goal displacement (Michels, 1949; Etzioni, 1964) indicate how articulated goals are replaced by other goals found to be more convenient. Goal displacement did not occur in precisely this way in the Cleveland project since the project never presented its task as the attainment of a set of specific goals. While a number of desirable goals were formulated and distributed in the planning documents, the project saw itself as a consciousness raiser and general integrator. An overview of the community after the project indicates that while some increased coordination and integration were achieved, important resistances to further integration also developed. That is, links between organizations increased, but, at the same time, these integrated organizations have probably increased their ability to resist additional communitywide integration.

Further, no central agency likely to achieve such coordination was established. Communication and coordination between organizations were provided by the Mental Retardation Committee or the Agency Forum during the project. But the bodies intended to continue central coordination, such as the Cuyahoga County Association for Retarded Children and the 648 Board, have put limitations on their scope and influence.

It had been assumed also that the Welfare Federation would continue to play a central role as a planner and coordinator of mental retardation services. However, no full-time staff person in the federation was assigned to retardation after completion of the project. The overall direction seemed to be reduction in the financial power of the federation and the increasing unlikelihood of its playing a dominant role in the retardation delivery system. Thus, if we consider the goal of the project to be the development of permanent communitywide coordination and integration, in an important sense that goal was displaced.

Factors affecting implementation of services. The project did little to prevent this outcome since it had opted early for a strategy of decentralization and no coercion. It attempted to make changes on a number of fronts simultaneously, and a partially linked system was one of the results. The project did not build into its design a method for bringing together the heads of agencies for regular interchange and cooperation on an ongoing basis. Nor did it develop a means for communitywide interagency collaboration or even communication, which could have assured joint planning and implementation and which could have continued after the demonstration project.

Further, the project did little to work on client-level coordination, that is, a system of case management or contracts for coordinated referrals. The project probably however contributed to the informal exchange of clients, both through increasing communication between agencies and through the information and referral service.

Even if the project did not directly contribute organizational structures that could play a strong role in coordination, are the lessons learned applicable to other situations? They are, if one's intentions are primarily to develop community concern, to exchange information, and to engage in policy discussion. Perhaps projects intended for only temporary results or aimed only at community awareness are best served by these methods. However, if one's intentions are long term and large scale and involve structural changes in a delivery system, such an approach may be less appropriate. Although the Cleveland project was constrained by the intention of the staff and the federation to use a community-organization approach emphasizing central communication and planning, the project could have used its limited resources to set up a permanent, formal communication and planning structure. This is not to say that one should aim at developing a powerful superagency all at once. However, the formalization of a communitywide structure, at whatever level, would perhaps have had a greater permanent effect than relying merely on informal communications structures.

Despite the drawbacks of the community-organization approach, we can gain from the project an appreciation of how independent agencies can be effectively handled. The project staff and committee did not attempt to force agencies to make large-scale program changes or to give up significant amounts of autonomy to a coordinating structure. They attempted rather to establish a centralizing influence of wide scope but low intensity. They made skillful use of their staff and committee structure in doing this and relied heavily on information gathering and sharing. Central to this communications effort was the planning document. Some agencies adjusted their programs in response to this document. And since the sixty-two goals were relatively general and took into account the major viewpoints in the retardation community, there was little challenge to them as community policy statements.

Routinization Stage

This project does demonstrate what can be accomplished even with an emphasis on only one component—information coordination.

7

Lessons for Service Delivery Systems

From the experiences of the five projects we can gain an understanding of their successes and failures, and from these comparisons we can discover general pitfalls and barriers in the development of coordinated services for the mentally retarded. In this and the following chapter we discuss some of these lessons as well as return to the change strategies briefly discussed in the first chapter. We also review the success of each project in obtaining resources for its activities, in mobilizing other organizations to join with it in common action, in developing programs, and in ensuring its survival. Throughout we are concerned primarily with coordination of the four elements which must be included in an integrated service delivery system: coordination of client needs, coordination of programs and services, coordination of community resources, and coordination of information.

Coordination in the Five Projects

San Francisco. The San Francisco project attempted to coordinate clients through the establishment of a case committee, on which participation was voluntary, and through the Information and Referral Service; but both were initiated before the grant was received and therefore were not directly a result of the project.

The project made a few attempts to coordinate the activities of agencies through joint programming. The test case, establishment of a day-care center, made manifest the latent competition among the agencies participating on the Coordinating Council on Mental Retardation (CCMR), and no further attempts at service delivery were made. The CCMR was able to mobilize informally members of most agencies serving the retarded in San Francisco, although there was attrition in the number of active participants over the five-year period. Some agency personnel participated in rezoning efforts coordinated by the CCMR, but this activity did not involve the agencies directly. The CCMR was successful in its efforts to establish a transportation plan, but none of the agencies was willing to commit its resources to implementing the plan, and additional funding was not obtained.

The San Francisco project made no attempt to coordinate funding either directly or indirectly. It also made little effort to obtain additional funding for the retarded directly. The absence of such an attempt is understandable, however, because after the attempt to provide seed money for the joint program on day care was thwarted, the project had difficulty putting even the funding that it had to good use.

The CCMR appeared to have legitimacy initially, even though participation was voluntary and informal. However, as the conflict among the agencies represented, especially between the parents organization and the professional organizations, began to show itself in work on specific efforts, the legitimacy of the organization with other agencies in the community declined.

The CCMR, like the Los Angeles project, worked extensively on the preparation of new state legislation for the retarded, the Lanterman Mental Retardation Act of 1969, and, like the Los Angeles project, it claimed to be influential in its passage. However, unlike the Los Angeles project, the CCMR was not undermined by the Lanterman Act. The CCMR continued in existence as the Developmental Disabilities Committee with the San Francisco Comprehensive Health Planning Council.

Bridgeport. Of the five projects, Bridgeport had the least communitywide focus as well as the smallest community upon which to focus. Consequently, this project is difficult to evaluate from the standpoint of creating a community service delivery system.

In program development this project performed similarly to the CCMR. The Parents and Friends of Mentally Retarded Children had as their first objective the collection of funds for the provision of services to their own children or children of friends. They wished either to perform these activities themselves or at least to retain stringent control over their provision. But, with the grant, professionals entered the picture, and they suggested services which the parents did not want to provide. The parents ultimately forced out those who would n t follow their wishes. Hence the structure established by this project was not conducive to program development, at least from a professional point of view. Energies were expended instead on hiring and firing staff and on all the consequences of doing so, such as monitoring activities of distrusted staff, training new staff, and resolving disagreements. Consequently, only a few programs were the concrete results of this project: Tri-Us, a workshop, and a residential-care program.

While the programs established under the project and by the parents group were coordinated with each other, these were only one segment of the services in the Bridgeport area which were specifically for the retarded or which multiproblem clients could use. Since the other services were not coordinated by the project and because well-forged links were not established with these programs, service coordination cannot be said to have been achieved.

The Parents and Friends, with their pre-grant structure, were a good fund-raising source for their own programs. But the project did nothing to coordinate funds within the whole community.

The coordination of clients was probably achieved well for those clients the project served. Outreach activities were attempted on behalf of other retarded in the area by the professionals, but parent-professional conflicts brought these activities to a halt. Consequently, the goal of communitywide coordination of clients was not met: all retarded were not reached, and the retarded within the program did not have their cases coordinated other than with those services under the auspices of the Parents and Friends.

Milwaukee. The focus of the Milwaukee project was on providing a continuum of care, a fixed point of referral, and case management for a limited number of clients in order to demonstrate the efficacy of these modes of service delivery. The project did not consider coordination of all services for the mentally retarded. It assumed that serving a few clients with a full range of services was better than serving all clients with unrealized plans.

The client-centered goals of the project make evaluation from a communitywide perspective difficult, but it is instructive to compare this project with others to see the adequacies of such an approach in the context of overall community needs. The private-agency auspices of the project was sufficient to keep it funded and to pick up extra operating expenses, but the agency, Jewish Vocational Service (JVS), lacked communitywide legitimacy to gather funds for provision of services to even a limited number of clients, much less to clients throughout the community. However, the change from private to public auspices brought limited success to the subsequent organization, the Agencies Integrated Delivery Service (AIDS), in obtaining funds from both government and a group of private agencies. Neither structure however was capable of generating much money since they were not designed or intended to do so.

In considering the mobilization of other organizations, remarks similar to those concerning the gathering of resources can be made. Few attempts were made by the Structured Community Services (SCS) project to gain cooperation, largely because initial attempts had resulted in little more than nominal participation of key agencies on the SCS board. Since the project was under the auspices of one of the major competitors of these other participating agencies, it is not surprising that other agencies hedged about referring their clients to it. With the coming of the AIDS program, however, the cost to each participating agency became a major stumbling block.

The strong point of the SCS project was in the development of programs. The project staff members were able to work in close conjunction with the staff of JVS, a service-providing agency, and hence they could easily locate gaps in services. Programs were easily implemented since project staff could rely on JVS to supply extra resources to launch them.

The project was not, however, able to initiate or to keep many of these programs going if they involved other agencies because it could provide no incentive to other agencies to cover their costs. The establishment of AIDS resulted largely from the efforts of the director of JVS and the incentive scheme funded by the federal government; but, nonetheless, AIDS would not have been undertaken at all without the demonstration by SCS of the usefulness of case-management techniques in coordinating services for multiple-disability clients. The SCS project did not coordinate services in the mental retardation field for the Milwaukee area, nor was this ever its intent. AIDS succeeded in coordinating services for the mentally retarded to the extent that several organizations both planned services for a limited group of clients and then delivered these services. These projects were most successful in the area of client coordination. The techniques of case management were developed and applied in such a way that a limited number of clients truly had available to them a continuum of care, which involved both delivery of services needed and, more important, monitoring of progress so that service delivery was tailored to individual needs. Despite the restricted number of clients, this project clearly demonstrated the feasibility and importance of case management.

Los Angeles. The Mental Retardation Services Board

(MRSB) in Los Angeles also coordinated some elements but not others. Its greatest potential was in coordinating resources and in establishing itself as a legitimate power base for the planning of service delivery by public agencies. Its weakness lay in the coordination of clients, which it did not consider its mandate.

The MRSB consisted of directors and highly placed staff members of service agencies, most of which were large and public. Few such agencies were not represented on the board. Hence, the board had access to a large amount of power and resources, although these were vested in its members rather than in the board itself. The board did not have to rely on voluntary contributions of money or manpower. For conducting a needs survey and for gaining access to information for planning purposes, the legitimacy of the board was of unquestioned value. Since the board was composed of agency directors, at least at the beginning, it was possible for these participants to commit their agencies to proposed courses of action. The board thus got to first base, although persuading the directors to maintain their participation or to commit their agencies to activities which involved spending money was another matter.

The structure established by the MRSB proved more ideal for gathering information and planning than it did for implementing new programs. The survey of services for the retarded and of the mentally retarded population and its distribution and the plan for coordinating community resources and services to cope with gaps, duplications, and other problems were well done, highly technical, filled with well-thought-out specific recommendations, and devoid of banal requests for greater effort or more coordination. But while the board assembled technical experts and produced an excellent plan, it was not able to translate this plan into action.

The board had some success in persuading the city school system to augment its services to the trainable retarded. It was also successful in stimulating several other multiple-agency projects. In some cases the MRSB was able to affect programs in particular agencies, even those that were not part of it, through the links the staff members had made with those agencies. Its effect on state legislation is unclear; it was one of several voices urging passage of the Lanterman bill. Finally, through the publication of its plan the board may have had an effect on numerous programs developed in the agencies in the area, but this effect was at best indirect.

The MRSB itself ceased to exist after the Lanterman legislation and the creation of the regional center at the Children's Hospital because its inflexible structure did not incorporate the private service sector. Also state legislators felt they wanted to establish the regional centers independently of the Mental Hygiene Department, which was heavily involved with the MRSB in Los Angeles and was responsible administratively for the large state hospitals. As a result the MRSB was not asked to participate in the regional coordination of services established by the state, and since its prime function was being performed elsewhere, it did not survive.

The impact of this program on the coordination of clients was almost nonexistent. The coordinated service delivery plan was ignored, and while some coordination of clients was done in the preschool program, the amount, considering the number of retarded in the area, was minimal.

In coordination of resources, the impact of this project was again mixed. The program succeeded in raising adequate resources for itself and in helping other agencies win contracts and grants to improve their services. The project had the potential to coordinate resources and was able to get some agencies to allocate an increased proportion of their funds to programs. But this potential was limited because the private sector was not adequately represented. If it had been, the structure would have been ideal for the communitywide coordination of resources, provided the agencies involved would have allowed it.

Cleveland. In Cleveland the project had little trouble establishing legitimacy because of its connections with the Welfare Federation and its highly competent staff, but the methods which its staff adopted vitiated efforts to bring about the coordination of services in the area. As long as the project confined itself to planning and did not attempt to influence service organizations in any way other than by demonstration and persuasion, its legitimacy remained high, but, because it had little clout, its effect on service delivery was unmeasurable and probably minimal.

Because of its ties with the Welfare Federation, the project had no trouble obtaining funds for its planning and information-dissemination activities. However, the project was unable to use money as an incentive to other organizations to develop cooperative programs because it had limited resources of its own and because it had little influence on the funding section of the Welfare Federation.

The project used its base within the Welfare Federation to put together a highly competent planning staff. The strategy they developed was first to assemble information and write up plans on the coordination of services and then to present them to other agencies with the hope that they would develop needed programs and coordinate services among themselves. During the developmental phase of the project, the Welfare Federation relied on the activity of two to three community organizers and on the centralization of communication through regular meetings of all the significant people in the retardation field, as well as on other assorted information-sharing activities.

It also developed two demonstration programs hoping that their success would encourage other organizations to pick them up. The first of these, the Mobile Analysis and Rehabilitation Team (MART), lasted until project funding was terminated and the workshops in the area refused to pick it up. The information and referral service, continued after the project, was a joint program of the Community Information Service and the local parents association for the retarded.

The project attempted little in the way of client coordination; it relied on persuasion of agencies to handle clients. Use of a more effective means of compliance would have depended on the United Appeal's allowing its funds to be used to entice or coerce agencies to participate in a client-coordination scheme, and this coordination would have been successful at best only with the private agencies. But even this plan was not attempted and probably would have been rejected by the United Appeal board in any case.

The participants felt they had an impact on the passage

of state legislation and state and county efforts to coordinate services, but others dispute this assessment and are willing to attribute to the project only a catalytic effect—the existence of the project probably hastened, but did not cause, this coordination. Since thorough coordination almost always requires drastic changes by agencies, communication and planning alone are not sufficient to achieve it. Coordination eventually costs money, and agencies must either be paid or be sanctioned to cooperate. State efforts and the subsequent creation of the 169 and 648 Boards provide an interesting contrast in methods of coordinating services. Here, insolvent and financially troubled workshops and schools for the retarded were funded by the state contingent upon their participation in the system.

The project cannot be said to have had a measurable impact on the coordination of resources in the community. Even the parent agency of the project, the Welfare Federation, which did control many resources, did not follow up the project and make an effort itself to engage in coordination of funding, despite project plans and persuasive actions in this area.

General problems. The foregoing comparisons of the five projects must be understood in context. Most projects do not accomplish what they set out to do, and the more innovative the project, the more this is true. Each of these demonstration projects tried to resolve fundamental issues—lack of services, fragmentation of services, and absence of coordination—which have seldom been satisfactorily solved in urban centers in the United States. Furthermore, in these urban contexts, the multiplicity of political jurisdictions, the variety of organizations, and the number of professional and parents associations lead to difficulties and conflicts which are not present in less complex environments. Finally, the projects frequently had insufficient financial resources. The surprising thing is that anything was accomplished.

In addition, there was a general lack of knowledge about how best to bring about coordination at the outset of these projects. Had those involved had greater knowledge and a fuller understanding of the problems, they might have changed their objectives. Hindsight however is always better than foresight, and criticism after the fact is obviously easier than choosing among alternatives with uncertain outcomes before the fact. Only in assembling this information about the different approaches and experiences of these projects and by comparing them have we been able to develop some insights about achieving coordinated service delivery.

The essential question for us is why the projects did not accomplish all they had wanted and, more important, how they might have done so. For each project, we have identified what we feel to be mistakes in the strategies utilized. In the rest of this chapter we analyze the delivery structures used by the five projects and some that were not. Then, in the final chapter, we outline a suggested optimal structure for avoiding similar mistakes in the future.

Service Delivery Structures

The most basic lesson regarding service delivery which can be learned from the experiences of these five projects is that particular structures are appropriate for coordinating some elements in a service delivery system (information, clients, programs and services, or resources), but inappropriate for coordinating other elements. When the service delivery structure does not match the element to be coordinated, it is highly unlikely to be successful. These two points are elaborated at length throughout this chapter.

From our perspective there are five basic service delivery structures (see Table 2):

(1) A network of service organizations coordinated by one organization in the network, using few or no formal links, but relying on voluntary cooperation alone. Although several of the projects attempted to form this loose type of service delivery system, their lack of success points out its ineffectiveness for bringing about coordinated service delivery as we have defined it in this book. Without extra funds or legal directives, organizations will not cooperate to any significant degree with the organizing efforts of a competitive organization. An example of this type of system is the Milwaukee project, which was

Table 2

Kinds of Service Delivery Structures and Elements to be Coordinated

Type of Organizational Structure or Form	Elements			
	Information[a]	Clients	Programs	Resources
(1) Single organization with some services for a multiproblem client	Equally effective	Ineffective	Ineffective	Ineffective
(2) Single organization with all services for a single multiproblem client	Equally effective	Most effective[b] or	Most effective[b]	Less effective
(3) Single organization with wide range of services for all clients	Equally effective	Most effective[c] or	Most effective[c]	Less effective
(4) Coalition of organizations for a single multiproblem client	Equally effective	Less effective	Most effective	Less effective
(5) Community board	Equally effective	Less effective	Less effective	Most effective

[a] Each form is likely to be as effective for information coordination as for coordination of the element it is most effective with.

[b] A single specialized organization—one handling all multiproblem clients of a particular kind—can coordinate clients or programs but not both equally effectively.

[c] A single organization designed to handle all clients needing physical, psychological, and social services can handle coordination of clients or of programs but not both equally effectively.

originally under the auspices of one private agency (JVS) which attempted to induce coordination of clients from other agencies.

(2) A single organization that provides case coordination and services for one kind of multiproblem client. As can be seen in Table 2, this form probably can be effective for the coordination of clients or for the coordination of programs but probably not both. The former pattern is the more typical possibility, as in some regional centers that do case coordination and purchase services. Other regional centers have tried to do both, but as we indicate later, there is an inherent conflict of interest; the interests of the clients are not likely to be protected when the same agency provides both case management and therapy.

(3) A single organization providing directly all the services that a given category of client needs. This form differs from the previous one in the variety of clients served. One can imagine, for example, an organization designed to serve all kinds of clients needing some form of rehabilitation. Again we speculate that such an agency can be effective with either case management or provision of services but not both. This type of organization differs significantly from those in all our projects, which were concerned with a single multiproblem client—the mental retardate. We have included this form for the sake of contrast and to broaden the range of the debate.

(4) A coalition of organizations, in which representatives from all the agencies giving services to a particular category of client formally band together and agree to manage joint programs to deal with the interdependent needs of the clients. The Los Angeles and Milwaukee (AIDS) projects approximated this structure, although the idea had not been developed previously in the literature. Such a coalition necessarily involves conflicts and tensions since it attempts to integrate the planning and supervision of programs of different service delivery organizations while keeping their organizational identities intact. Realistically, the only way such a coalition can stay together is if some outside source, most likely the federal government, provides a substantial amount of funds or other resources to member agencies as a condition of participation. Such an ongoing,

formal coalitional structure encourages joint programming and other forms of cooperation, but at the same time it preserves organizational identities and traditions and is not likely to threaten organizational needs for autonomy. An important and distinguishing characteristic of the coalition is that organizations and not just individual professionals or administrators are members. Each organization sends to periodic meetings official representatives who have the authority to commit their organizations to cooperative uses of funds, staff, or facilities. The two most appropriate people to represent the organization are the executive director and the program director if these positions are held by different persons, as is usually the case. The executive director has sufficient formal authority, and the program director has the required expertise.

(5) A formally constituted board of individuals from the community representing various interest groups, classes, or institutions. Perhaps the best example of this organizational form is that in Cleveland, where there was a deliberate attempt to have representation of different collective interests from the community; the Los Angeles board also represented different organizational interests from the community. This organizational form differs from those previously discussed in that the coordination of services is provided not by a service delivery organization as such, but rather by a board, the primary responsibility of which is policy making and resource procuring. The service delivery system, however, is likely to be one of the structures already discussed.

These five delivery structures are not simply points along a continuum of one dimension, however. Three primary dimensions are implicit in this typology: the variety of clients dealt with, the amount of integration of elements in the system, and the level at which coordination is attempted. This latter point is critical and needs elaboration. Organizations in a community operate on at least three different levels: treatment of clients by service-giving professionals (the professional level), program planning and coordination by top administrators (the managerial level), and resource allocation for the total delivery system (the institutional level). A basic hypothesis of this book is that there is an appropriate level at which each element (resources, programs and services, clients, information) is best coordinated. Resources, principally funds, are best coordinated at the institutional level, which means the community level when dealing with community service delivery systems. Programs and services are best coordinated at the managerial level. The clients are best coordinated at the professional level through case management. Information needs to be coordinated at all levels, although different types of information are appropriately coordinated at different levels. We argue that the projects made two major errors: They attempted to coordinate particular elements at the wrong levels, and they did not attempt to coordinate all four elements equally. Each project generally chose an intervention point—namely, the level at which the formal authority of the project could be exerted—which was inappropriate for the particular element the project focused on. This may seem an obvious point, but it was not well understood by the participants at the outset of these five projects. Therefore, we think it useful to outline the experiences of these projects to demonstrate what in hindsight may seem like common sense.

The Bridgeport sponsor, a single organization, was most successful in managing services to the clients under its jurisdiction. When the professionals working on the project attempted to extend the authority of the organization to include new clients, difficulties arose. The professionals did not have formal authority and so had to resign when the major clash occurred. Because this project did not get to the point of attempting to coalesce with other agencies, it is not clear what success they might have had. Given the San Francisco experience, other agencies would probably have been suspicious of too much formal alignment with a parents organization. The strategy chosen by this project and the structure of the project matched. When the strategy began to shift toward other organizations, conflict resulted and the project was halted. The project did not attempt to create a community board or a coalition of organizations.

The San Francisco project had the formal authority of a single organization, but informally attempted to act as a coalition of organizations. Its most successful efforts were those involving the coordination of clients. It set up a case-coordination committee which operated on a voluntary basis and was quite successful at coordinating information. At this level, the strategy of the San Francisco project matched its structure. However, the San Francisco project also attempted to create several programs which would have involved a coalition of organizations. These programs included the aborted day-care project, the aborted zoning effort, and the unimplemented transportation project. As a single organization without formal authority from the agencies represented to commit funds in a highly competitive environment, the project was totally unsuccessful at coordinating programs and services. These efforts mismatched the formal authority (single organization) and the focus of coordination (programs and services of other organizations), even though the project informally attempted to act as a coalition. The only attempt by the San Francisco project at coordinating resources was in its planning for the Lanterman Act. Again, the leverage of a single organization was not successful. Therefore, in order to accomplish the Lanterman planning, the CCMR had to contract out to a "neutral" research organization, one not in the system and even outside the county.

The first phase of the Milwaukee project, the SCS program, was designed to be a single organization but tried to act as a coalition of organizations both in coordinating clients and in coordinating programs. It was able to coordinate its own clients and to develop some programs for them but not to coordinate clients of other organizations or to get competitors to create new programs for the clients. In this way it functioned much like the Bridgeport project even though it tried much longer to reach out into the larger community. The committee involving other agencies was correctly perceived as a public relations device and did not elicit meaningful cooperation. In attempting to operate as a formal coalition without formal authority, the project was unsuccessful in coordinating clients because the agencies participating declined to share their clients. In this phase, then, the structure (informal coalition) did not match the focus (client management). It was necessary for the Milwaukee project to move to a second phase and create a formal coalition of organizations before the participating agencies were willing to share their clients.

As a coalition of organizations with a focus on client management, the AIDS program was somewhat successful in generating referrals from participating agencies as long as those agencies could care for the clients themselves; the mismatch between the structure (a coalition of organizations) and the focus (client management) resulted in serving fewer clients than a single agency might have been able to do. The coalition was unsuccessful in generating enough money to achieve active participation from some of the competitors. The Milwaukee project did not attempt to coordinate resources for the whole community; if it had, it would not have been successful.

The structure of the Los Angeles project was that of a community board, but one where the members were organizations. Although there was a formal contract, the contract was just an agreement to agree and thus lacked formal force. The project was most successful when it attempted to generate additional resources. Because the MRSB did not include all agencies in the community (it did not include most private agencies or representatives of minority groups), it was not as successful in coordinating programs and services. And, in any case, the agencies which participated agreed to join together to provide a base for bargaining with outside structures, not to coordinate their own programs and services. Some efforts at program coordination were successful, but the number of such efforts was minimal; it was especially difficult to coordinate services with nonparticipating agencies such as the private hospital chosen to be the regional center. The Los Angeles project made little attempt to do case management. It thus was matched in structure and focus for the purposes of those agencies involved; however, it was not sufficiently broad in that it did not include enough of the community.

The Cleveland project operated as a community board but did not attempt to coordinate resources among the agencies providing services to the mentally retarded in the community. Although the project did fund several new service programs (for example, MART), it also did not attempt to directly coordinate

them with other agencies in the community. Rather, the board
chose to develop standard procedures which were to be voluntarily adopted by community agencies. However, because the
project could not, and did not wish to, ensure that local agencies would follow these procedures, little was accomplished on
this level. The Cleveland project made one attempt to coordinate clients through client management (a community information service), but as in the Milwaukee project, this program
serviced only a small number of clients. The staff of the Cleveland project focused primarily on the coordination of information, and this it did quite well. However, the project could have
been even more successful had it chosen to focus on the coordination of resources, where it did have some leverage as part of a
prestigious community board.

These projects illustrate some of the pitfalls encountered
in attempting to coordinate elements at the wrong level or in
excluding one or more elements from coordination efforts. In
the next section we examine generally the inherent effectiveness
of each alternative structure for coordinating the various elements.

Alternative Delivery Systems

Because of the nature of the five projects described,
there are two fundamental limitations on the range of alternatives considered here. First, four of the five projects occurred in
metropolitan areas which had one million or more people and
which were among the largest twenty metropolitan areas in
1970. Thus, with the exception of Bridgeport, these projects
attempted to bring about coordination of services in areas characterized by a relatively high degree of governmental fragmentation. Second, all these demonstration projects involved attempts
to bring about greater coordination of services for one type of
multiproblem client—the mentally retarded. Hence, our observations must apply primarily to large metropolitan areas and only
to the multiproblem client. While some of the observations
below may be relevant to smaller population centers and to
single-disability client populations, we suggest some caution in
generalizing our discussion to these situations.

Even for the multiproblem client, these five demonstration projects do not represent all the possible organizational arrangements. As is usually true in the case of quasiexperiments, the funding agency (the VRA, now called Social and Rehabilitation Services of the Department of Health, Education, and Welfare) was unable to cover all ways of establishing auspices as well as the consequent organizational arrangements. In part this lack of coverage occurred because of a decision to fund only a limited number of projects, but, more important, the VRA was dependent upon who applied or who could be induced to apply.

The purpose of this section, therefore, is to examine some alternative delivery systems for the multiproblem client in an urban setting, as well as to speculate about what might be the best delivery strategy for maximizing the coordination (cooperation, compatibility, comprehensiveness) of each of the elements we have identified as being essential parts of a service delivery system: resources, programs and services, clients, and information. Naturally we would like to find an alternative that is the best of all possible worlds, one that not only maximizes coordination of the four essential elements of a service delivery system, but also includes mechanisms to ensure accessibility and accountability.

As we noted in the first chapter, while resources, programs and services, and clients can be conceived as being on three vertical levels of the delivery system, information crosscuts all three of these levels, especially since, as we pointed out, both internal and external aspects of information must be considered. From the internal perspective, a service delivery system would include feedback mechanisms to obtain information about the operation of the system at all three levels—how well clients were being serviced, how well programs and services were being coordinated, how available and well utilized resources were. For this reason, we concentrate at this point on the coordination of the three vertical aspects of service delivery systems: resources, programs and services, and clients.

The projects were chosen primarily on the basis of their auspices: a parent group in Bridgeport, a private organization in Milwaukee, a voluntary association of professionals in San

Francisco, a traditional private welfare federation in Cleveland, and a joint powers agreement among a variety of governmental and other agencies in Los Angeles. While auspices is important and did have a profound effect on some of these projects, auspices primarily determines policy making in and governance of the organizational entity that attempts to coordinate services. Equally important is what kind of organizational structure is best suited for executing or implementing the coordination of service delivery. In the discussion that follows therefore we examine the five different organizational arrangements for the coordination of service delivery and cover problems of policy making as well as of policy implementation.

In this section we attempt to answer two questions: First, which of these organizational forms is best designed to achieve coordination of the various elements? Second, and equally important, how is it possible to achieve the coordination of all the elements we have identified in the same structure?

Besides attempting to answer these questions, this section also deals with design issues which were raised only tangentially in our five case studies. A review of the literature on service delivery indicates that the themes of accessibility and accountability are given as much attention and considered to be as important as the three aspects of coordination—cooperation, compatibility, and comprehensiveness. We have chosen to place more emphasis at the outset on coordination because we feel that the problem of coordination is more critical than these other issues. It does not make much sense to discuss accessibility and accountability unless there are adequate programs and resources for which accessibility and accountability are problematic. In addition, the issues involved in the concept of coordination as defined here were the major concerns of the projects, and rightly so.

Another one of the popular themes in the literature on service delivery systems is the integration of all services for all clients, a possibility alluded to in our discussion of the third of these organizational forms above. In our discussion of the ideal delivery system here, however, we first discuss service delivery systems for multiproblem clients. We consider that integrated social services are difficult to achieve for clients such as these, given current constraints and commitments, and hence we prefer to consider the issues involved in creating coordinated service delivery structures for multiproblem clients before discussing the more complex problem of whether it is desirable or advantageous to combine all service delivery into a single integrated system. Once we have discussed the problems of coordination, accountability, and accessibility in service delivery systems for a particular kind of multiproblem client, then we can briefly consider whether our proposal for an ideal service delivery system is feasible for all clients who need some rehabilitation or maintenance and support.

We are discussing both the type of delivery system and the best fit in ideal-typical terms. But pure forms never occur in reality. There will always be some mixture of these types in any particular setting. Many subtleties and variations in these systems are not captured by these categories. We are predicting which structure will probably maximize the coordination of the four elements rather than suggesting that coordination will be totally or largely absent under various structural arrangements. We have found that the delineation of these four elements has greatly clarified our own thinking about the problems of coordinated service delivery systems since approaching the problem in this way suggests that one organizational form, or an aspect of it, may be necessary for coordinating one element, but another is necessary for coordinating another element. We have encountered only one writer who makes such distinctions (Reid, 1964). We hope to be able to show that these distinctions are not always mutually exclusive, but, on the contrary, some combination of them is necessary if coordinated service delivery is to be forthcoming.

Single organization with few formal links. Our suggestion that a single organization with few formal links is ineffective in creating a coordinated delivery system in a community with many competing organizations is well documented by our case studies. Most single organizations do not have sufficient resources to induce other organizations to participate in joint programs and share clients if the other organizations must give up substantial amounts of their autonomy. Not only are organizations often suspicious of each other, but as we suggested in an earlier chapter they also jealously guard their autonomy. The example in the first phase of the Milwaukee project is again especially relevant. The other major rehabilitation agencies in Milwaukee were attracted to the goals of the program but were unwilling to cooperate as long as the funding was solely under the control of JVS. Thus, our conclusion is that a single organization can best maximize coordination of its own clients among its own departments. Precisely because an organization has limited programs and resources, it is better for it to concentrate on providing high quality services to a limited range of clients, rather than wasting resources on what we feel are futile efforts to coordinate the services of other organizations.

Single organization with all services for a multiproblem client. Discussion of the single organization that provides all services for a particular kind of multiproblem client is difficult without recognizing that one of the services is case management. Our position is that a single organization can do the case management for a multiproblem client or do the therapy but not both. In general, we believe that the single organization is best suited for case management with purchase of all necessary services, especially when the multiproblem client has a wide variety of needs that are met by a number of different agencies. When the client's needs are limited and of short duration, as, for example, in most kinds of illnesses, then an organization such as a hospital works well (Lefton and Rosengren, 1966). However, as the duration and the variety of the needs increase, the combination of therapy and case management in the same authority structure becomes difficult.

An advantage of a single organization is that the single entry point (fixed point of referral) minimizes the possibility that clients will get "lost." A coalition, with multiple entry points, or a board which does not directly deliver services obviously could not perform this function as well. This does not mean that a board or a coalition of organizations could not create an organizational unit or suborganizational unit to provide case coordination. However, if the agency that provides case coordination also provides services, there is a possibility of a conflict of interest, namely, that a single organization would act as its own watchdog. In this arrangement, the clients often lose out. Thus, a case-coordination unit would itself have to have some autonomy from the agency of which it was a part in order to perform the function of case management, or it would have to be a separate agency from the service agency. Service delivery personnel are often concerned with only one problem of the multiproblem client. The advantage of separating case management from delivery is that the case manager is able to assess all the needs of his client.

Another advantage of locating responsibility for case coordination in a single organization is that it simplifies considerably record-keeping problems. The case coordinator can keep one set of records on a multiproblem client receiving services from several agencies. A single organization assuming responsibility for client coordination also will keep an up-to-date directory of services that are available. Furthermore, when case coordination is assigned to a single agency, the problem of comprehensiveness can be addressed because that organization will likely develop techniques for identifying and locating all clients.

Putting all therapeutic services for a single multiproblem client under one roof involves several possible dangers. The most critical is that one profession or therapeutic approach might become dominant. The consequence would be unbalanced growth as new technological breakthroughs occurred. The great advantage, however, is that coordination of programs is under a single authority structure, and economies of scale can be achieved.

An important element in resource coordination is whether the right amount of funds is given to the right agencies or programs or both. Locating resource coordination in a single agency is not likely to resolve this problem because the biases and needs of this agency will result in a myopic view of how scarce resources should be allocated.

Another problem with having a single organization coordinate resources is that many other organizations do not allow another organization to dictate policies. While the power of the

purse may be a necessary condition for control, it is not a sufficient one. When organizations are asked to give up programs,
they are not likely to do so, even if faced with severe reductions
in funding. An extreme example of this occurred in Milwaukee
when a district office of vocational rehabilitation cut off most
funds to one sheltered workshop. This cut-off resulted in a one-
fifth reduction in payroll and a subsequent reduction in staff,
but not one program was discontinued. Programs are always
justifications for future funding. Thus, a specialized service
organization is probably not the most appropriate one for the
coordination of services or the elimination of duplicate services.

Perhaps the most severe problem with placing all funding
in a single specialized agency is that, even if it has a determined
supporting clientele, it does not usually have enough votes to
obtain a larger share of the taxes, to say nothing about being
able to increase taxes. Thus, it is unlikely to have enough
money to help all the needy clients and to provide them with
enough services. This lack of money can affect the comprehensiveness of clients served and of services provided.

We must distinguish two different situations which we
mentioned at the beginning of this discussion. In one, there is
disbursement of funds but no direct provision of services. In the
other, the organization disbursing the funds also provides services. In the former situation, the dynamics are to encourage
service duplication so that the organization purchasing them has
a choice. Therefore, competition is encouraged. In the latter
situation, the dynamics are for the organization to keep the
money for itself rather than to spend it in purchasing services
from the other agencies in the delivery system. Once this
occurs, we have not only duplication but the creation of a large
agency that is likely to spend most of the money for its own
services. This situation facilitates neither comprehensiveness of
programs nor compatibility. Resource coordination can occur
within a single organization, but pressures may prevent the
elimination of duplicate services even in one agency. Some
experts on social welfare consider duplication of services desirable (Landau, 1969), but one suspects that this is from the vantage point of how our present system operates.

Once case management and service delivery are under the

same roof, the possibilities for representing the interests of the client may be reduced, as we have suggested. Organizational interests are likely to dominate over client interests, unless outside advocacy groups can bring their influence to bear. This can and does occur in services to the blind, for example (R. A. Scott, 1969). Parents groups can perform this advocacy function by participating in the service delivery system while maintaining relative autonomy from it, for example by supporting case-coordination efforts. A problem with combining resource control and program control is that particular professions (for example, medicine) could become more powerful than others and thus generate more funds for their own programs than for others.

If this reasoning is correct, it suggests that parents groups and other voluntary associations representing the interests of multiproblem clients can play a useful role by using their scarce resources in supporting case coordination. Case coordination is a means of filling a major lacuna in many service delivery systems. Supporting this activity rather than recreational activities could result in greater leverage over scarce resources. Supporting case coordination should make parents groups or other associations aware of gaps in services as well as other problems in the delivery system, thus allowing them to maintain their advocacy role and to protect the clients who are frequently forgotten in the service delivery system.

Single organization providing services for all kinds of clients. This model attempts to house all services for all clients—unemployed, blind, retarded, indigent, mentally ill—in one administrative structure. Again, we find it useful to make a critical distinction between case management and direct services or therapy. We believe that a superagency can do one or the other but not both for the reasons provided above. Much of the present discussion about integration of services (March, 1968; Kronick, Perlmutter, and Gummer, 1973; O'Donnell and Reid, 1972) is probably focusing on some variation of this model, but the distinction we have made is critical in evaluating the proposals, for there is an important difference between integrating all case management and integrating all therapies.

The advantage of the superagency is in the simplification

of record keeping and economies of scale in services. Possibly, a relatively autonomous case-coordination unit within the organization could serve a large number of clients. Since such a model of service delivery does not necessarily imply geographical centralization, there could be a central unit with satellites scattered through the community, the central unit providing specialized services and the satellites providing intake, diagnosis, and generalized services. Such satellites have sometimes been referred to as neighborhood centers to suggest that service delivery should be integrated into the fabric of urban subcommunities if they are to be effective.

Some other advantages that would be available from this model of service delivery include the possibility of a central point of referral (a major goal of most of our projects), the possibility of flexibility in the services delivered if categorical funding were avoided in the budgets of such agencies, and, because of economies of scale, the possibility that either additional clients could be served or additional programs could be provided with the savings in cost. In addition, because such a single organization with multiple services would necessarily be an extremely complex organization, it would also be likely to be more innovative (Hage and Aiken, 1967; Aiken and Hage, 1968). Both joint programs and teams of specialists could easily be provided in this system. Perhaps a major advantage would be that the problems of interorganizational coordination would become problems of intraorganizational coordination among departments of the same organization and thus probably more manageable.

There are a number of difficulties with this structure however. Since it would be a single organization, even though offering diverse services, one or two professional specialties (such as medical or psychological) might become dominant and thus contribute to a lopsided service delivery without alternative sources of service available. There is a certain paradox here. Although we do believe that such a complex structure, if decentralized in its decision making, could be innovative, we are not completely convinced it would necessarily be innovative in all areas. Gaps in service might develop, especially with technological advances, and these gaps might never be filled since those in control of the superagency would be from a different professional specialty and would have no interest in filling them. Further, a single agency, even though large, could become politically vulnerable because it provides a single target. However, it would also simplify the accountability problems from the point of view of client representative groups; they could focus on one source of authority rather than a number of different authority structures.

One of the major problems with such a proposal is that if too many services are concentrated in a single organization for a wide variety of clients, the overall amount of financial resources available could be reduced since a single organization receiving funds for a wide variety of clients and services would perhaps be more politically vulnerable than a host of competing organizations, each with its special clientele, political supporters, and institutionalized arrangements.

However, the most difficult problem of all would probably be the changes which would have to be made in existing service delivery agencies within communities. Existence of a superagency could perhaps mean reduction of the private sector, reduction in the number of separate jurisdictions for hospitals (whether general or mental), and elimination of other organizational entities. Even minor reorganizations in such organizations are extremely difficult, primarily because of their autonomous tendencies. From a political point of view, it might be easier to create a single organization to service a single kind of multiple-problem client. However, it might be politically more feasible to create a single public organization that would do case management, as we have described it above. Because an agency can be more easily convinced to give up one service or program than to give up its autonomy and perhaps become a division of a larger organization, we suspect there might be some receptivity to this proposal.

Coalition of organizations. If a single organization—either specialized or general—can provide effective case coordination, a coalition of organizations is likely to be ineffectual in achieving this task, unless it establishes a single organization to perform it, as in the AIDS project in Milwaukee. Without a fixed point of referral and management of clients, there is no fixed responsibility, and clients never have access to a full array of services and a continuum of care. Referrals of clients among organizations and the consequent problems are well illustrated in the example at the beginning of Chapter One and are too numerous to list here. Referrals are not always made; if they are, they are not always accepted; client records are not passed along from one agency to the next; and, more important, each organization may view the client only from its vantage point. In the case of a single minor handicap, this may be less of a problem, but for a multiple-handicap person, piecemeal treatment is a disaster. Oddly enough, coalitions also do not assure location and identification of all potential clients because, without a single organization acting as a fixed point of referral, there is no place to refer clients for the handling of all needs, and thus the client is left to wander in a maze; in this sense, the client is never treated as having multiple problems.

In the coordination of programs, particularly in developing new programs to fill gaps in service, a coalition of organizations, if it has the necessary funds, is likely to be as effective as a single organization. But, in a coalition of organizations, there is much less opportunity for a single ideology or treatment philosophy to dominate. Each organization is represented by a single executive director, and thus the head of a sheltered workshop has no more to say than does the head of a special education department in the school system. Admittedly, because of personalities or the prestige of the organizations represented, some individuals may become more influential than others, but the formal equality of representation on the coalition committee should assure that no one professional specialty totally dominates another. The dynamics should encourage joint programming and the development of cooperative links between all specialties.

Another reason an organizational coalition may be one of the best ways to develop a continuum of care is that only certain organizations within the coalition may be powerful enough to get the funds needed. Organizations successful at getting funds can support organizations unsuccessful at getting funds but providing needed services.

Further, the coalition may encourage program coordination since both executive directors and program directors are represented on the board. Presumably if there is a great deal of task interdependence between the various organizations, as we suspect there is with multiproblem clients, this interdependence requires information feedback and joint planning at the program level, and program directors are involved in this planning. The regular interaction between program directors on the committee both makes them aware of the need for coordination and provides the arena for the working out of such coordination. The executive directors provide the needed authority to make organizational commitments to the cooperative arrangements that are worked out.

But there are some problems with a coalition. The major one is that a coalition may generate a tremendous amount of conflict by bringing together agency representatives with diverse ideologies, competing interests, and different personalities. Communication does not always resolve conflict; it may also intensify it by making potential antagonists aware of divergent interests. We do not evaluate all conflict negatively; indeed we argue that it is necessary for creative program development. However, we do recognize the possibility of destructive levels of conflict, and there is a potential for such conflict in a coalition.

A further problem is that an organizational coalition is unlikely to eliminate service duplication, which would require considerable collective self-discipline. Competitors could be expected to agree to expand their services simultaneously, but not to eliminate them.

A more subtle problem is whether a coalition of organizations can decide that, given the costs of particular services, some programs should have more money. As soon as an agency claimed it was doing more for the client or handling the especially difficult cases, the other agency heads would discount it. Thus, the coordination of resources is a too difficult job for a coalition of executive directors. They can easily perceive gaps in service, the need for a continuum of care, and the desirability of task interdependence, but not necessarily the need to reallocate funds or staff or both in particular ways, which are issues of resource coordination.

Community board. Community boards tend to be ineffective with both case coordination and the development of a complete continuum of services because of a lack of expertise and a lack of time. Most boards meet only once a month, and they are usually made up largely of economic and political elites, not social-service professionals. Community boards sometimes have a mixture of professionals and local leaders, but, in general, not all areas of expertise are represented. Obviously a board cannot provide client coordination unless it creates a unit under its control to carry out this function.

The experience of the board in Cleveland and the board in Los Angeles suggests that community boards may also be less effective than a coalition of organizations in developing new programs and services because community boards are further removed from the day-to-day problems of creating joint programs and new services and completing the continuum of care. Here professionals and, more importantly, heads of organizations are likely to play a critical role because they can more easily commit their organizations, handle problems of resistance to change, and manage interagency conflicts.

The board is best designed to handle problems of service duplication. Boards function best in resolving interorganizational conflicts and working out compromises between organizations. The members of a board are much more likely to be sensitive to demands for efficiency than are heads of organizations and therefore are more interested in the elimination of duplicate services. And providing the critical match between resource and need is also something a board can do most effectively.

However, community boards, depending upon how they are structured, are likely to be most successful in generating funds. This is a traditional function and the one that most board members expect to play. They are experienced in putting pressure on legislators, mobilizing community support when necessary, and acting as intermediaries. Even if the private sector plays a decreasingly important role in the future in service delivery, the public sector may require similar kinds of boards in order to ensure legitimacy, accountability, and guidance. The board concept could also be superimposed on a coalition of organizations, as it could be (and often is) on the specialized, single-purpose organization.

These last comments imply that one kind of strategy is to combine structures. A large number of such alternatives could be discussed. Furthermore, the combinations of the separate structures should have the same strengths, and avoidances of weaknesses, of their constituent elements.

As we mentioned earlier, five different types of organizational structures can be used to provide coordination in a service delivery system. The first three are based on a single organization. The fourth structure involves a coalition of organizations, and the fifth a community board. In our analysis of these five types (in fact, of only four since we judged one ineffective for any type of coordination), we showed that each is adequate for coordination of some but not all elements (resources, programs, clients, information). Further, we pointed out that in the five projects two or more of these structures existed side by side in each community.

One possible fully comprehensive system would center around a large agency providing a full range of services for a given category of client. In its most developed form, it would have a full range of clients—it would be, in other words, a complete human services superagency. If this one structure were taken to its logical extreme, it would leave no room for any other service agency. But it is not economically or administratively possible to include all services for even one category of client. Services which are needed infrequently or which require highly specialized skills cannot be economically provided by a large agency. Attempts to provide all services would lead to needless duplication.

Further, even if it were possible to provide all services in the large superagency, it is not always desirable to do so from a treatment perspective. Many client problems stem from social isolation and stigma, and these might be increased by complete isolation of clients from other individuals who need the same services. The retarded, for instance, can make use of a wide variety of services and facilities also used by those with normal IQs, and no purpose is served by providing all these services through a large superagency.

Given these objections, it would seem that the large superagency should supply only the more general, routinized services and leave the highly specialized ones to separate organizations or individual practitioners. A need thus is created to coordinate programs, clients, and resources of many organizations, and thus a coalition and purchase-of-service unit are still needed to assure thorough coordination.

A large superagency would also have an equal if not greater need for a community board than would many separate organizations. The cost of such an agency would be large and quite visible, an easy target for groups critical of excessive expenditures or unpopular programs. Thus, an active and powerful board would be needed to maintain public support. Large state university systems are similar in the amount of funding and frequent unpopularity of programs, and their citizen boards seem necessary in maintaining support. In addition, a large agency would present great problems of public accountability. A board representing various segments of the population would provide channels of public influence and control over the operations of the agency.

Thus a large service-providing organization, in combination with a coalition, purchase-of-service unit, and a board, is one possibility. It would be comprehensive, would provide administrative channels for sequencing services, and could promote cooperation between the various service units as a matter of organizational policy. One disadvantage of this arrangement is simply its utopian character, given the current fragmentation of services in American communities and the political barriers to administrative merger.

A better and simpler strategy is one that combines three structures—a case-coordination unit, a coalition of organizations, and a community board. In Chapter One, we suggested that the ideal delivery system should have coordination of clients, programs, resources, and information. From this analysis, we see that we need to have these elements combined. Thus, our proposed strategy, discussed in the next chapter, is a synthesis of service delivery forms, combining their strengths and eliminating their weaknesses.

8

Creating Coordinated
Delivery Systems

In suggesting an ideal service delivery system, we make three assumptions. First, we assume that because clients with multiple problems, such as the mentally retarded, need a number of different services, joint programming or at least coordination of programs is required. Second, we assume the existence of interest groups that advocate the provision of services or at least advocate a recognition of the need for services. Third, we assume that we are discussing urban systems. In rural areas low case loads may require a different arrangement from the one proposed here.

Proposed Structure

Our essential hypotheses have been that coordination of clients is best done at an organizational level, that coordination of programs can occur either at the organizational level or with a coalition of organizations, and that coordination of resources

170

is best achieved at the community or board level. Thus the preferred alternative would be some combination of these structures to achieve complete coordination in the service delivery system. Because we have argued that the combination of case management and therapy in the same organization leads to a conflict of interest, we are concerned mainly with structures that keep these two components separate.

For us, an appropriate structure contains three key elements: a unit to do case coordination, a coalition of organizations, and a community board. The first element needs little discussion; the AIDS project provides one model. But the creation of a coalition of organizations and a community board requires explanation.

Coalition of organizations. Because joint programs require joint funding and because funding that goes to a single organization creates fear about loss of autonomy, agencies, both public and private, should be encouraged to operate as a team. Since the coalition would be funded collectively, the executive directors, with the approval of the board, should collectively make the decisions as to how the money should be allocated.

Here the main objective is comprehensiveness—to develop all the new services needed to provide a continuum of care. Attaining this objective requires the sustained interaction of the heads of agencies. If an organization can thus achieve program and resource coordination along with a comprehensive list of services and enough resources to support them, then information by definition is sufficiently coordinated. Joint funding of a coalition of organizations creates a structural imperative for information flow in the system and especially between competitors, where the barriers are the greatest (Warren, Rose, and Bergunder, 1974).

Operationally, organizational coalitions would work so that, for example, a sheltered workshop would develop specialized services for multiple-handicap clients in conjunction with the school system. Both the schools and the sheltered workshop would still provide their traditional services, but would develop new programs for new clients jointly. The investment, and thus the risk, on the part of each agency would be kept to a minimum since only some of the programs or services of the agency would be involved in the new delivery system.

A large number of problems are involved in implementing such an arrangement. One of the greatest difficulties is creating sufficient coordination so that programs articulate without making inconsistent demands on the client. Organizations have different concepts of treatment and staffs have different ideologies. We have argued that this diversity is healthy and results in a rich technological armentarium, but this diversity must be coordinated. Task interdependence creates many role conflicts for staff that must somehow be managed, so there are problems not only of external coordination but of internal coordination as well.

An important argument for the coalition of organizations is that it can obtain sufficient funding for the additional services necessary to provide a continuum of care. An organizational coalition involving public and private, symbiotic and competitive agencies is a powerful interest group state legislators and county commissioners have difficulty arguing against, especially if the coalition is combined with a community board. Furthermore, a coalition can enlist a wide variety of supporting client groups.

Earlier we argued that a coalition provides the interorganizational links to coordinate technologically interdependent services. It is also likely that coalitions will create interdependence by helping generate new service techniques that are responsive to the complex interrelationships of the clients themselves. Thus a coalition may accelerate the movement toward interdependence and, it is hoped, toward increased effectiveness in serving multiproblem clients (White, 1971; Warren, 1971).

However, the number of agencies that should be involved in a coalition is problematical. Very large cities such as Los Angeles have many agencies, not all of which can function effectively in a coalition. Therefore, we would expect that some rationalization would have to occur. For example, if there are a hundred suburban school districts, the county may become responsible for all mental retardation and represent these districts in a coalition. Likewise, an agency that handles just a few clients need not be involved at all.

Community board. A community board is necessary to protect the public interest. One arrangement would include equal numbers of community elites, professionals in areas relevant to the multiproblem client, and individuals representing the interests of the consumer or client. In suggesting this arrangement, we attempt to recognize various community power groups (who can provide resources) and to avoid focusing on only one or another interest group, as was the case in all the demonstration projects. There is sometimes a reluctance to admit that community elites exist and especially to state that their interests should be represented. From a power perspective, this denial seems unwise. Elites in a community can block efforts to obtain resources, and thus they should be involved from the outset. A denial of the existence of the power structure is no more realistic than a denial of the abuse of clients by professionals or a denial of the lack of expertise of most nonprofessionals. It may be necessary to legislate the composition of community boards in order to ensure balanced representation. This is what occurred in California, and it had significant effects on both the projects there.

Each of these interest groups also represents different values. Community elites emphasize efficiency and reduction of costs. Professionals are most concerned about quality care, and representatives of the consumers are concerned about the social-emotional needs of the consumer. Representation of different values on the board makes the delivery system accountable on more than one criterion. Accountability only on the criterion of efficiency results in a considerable reduction in quality of service and vice versa, for example.

Hopefully a dialogue can be created among these interests. Each group needs a check on its power, but it also needs a forum in which to present its viewpoint. A synthesis of perspectives should result from this dialogue. Equal representation in numbers does not necessarily imply equal representation of viewpoints. Some interests may be more influential and better able to have their wishes carried out. The value of our suggestion is that equal representation of various interest groups at least provides the opportunity to overcome some inequities and to begin the process of coordination.

This proposal resolves two practical problems often associated with boards: gaining political support and making membership on the board meaningful. If the three main interest groups are represented, then it seems likely that political support can be obtained. And if legislators provide support, membership becomes meaningful.

A community board also provides legitimacy for the organizations involved. Governments and community chests are presently reluctant to fund coalitions of organizations. They prefer the fixed responsibility of either a single organization or a single board. Community boards can provide the political support which is necessary if organizations are to engage the larger environment and gain resources from it. The community board can spend large amounts of time trying to get money, staff, and prestige for the service delivery system.

The tasks of the community board would be exactly those of any corporate board: to make policies about interorganizational relationships, transfers and exchanges, joint programming, and the like, and to protect the interests of the community regarding the allocation of funds. The boards would not plan or coordinate programs. These tasks would be left to the coalition of organizations to work out on their own subject to approval by the board.

When each multiproblem client is served by separate organizations, then there would be a separate board for each type of client. Likewise, if each type of client is served by a coalition, there would have to be as many coalitions as types of clients. With this arrangement, it is probable that any single organization would be part of several coalitions, depending upon the range of the services offered by that particular organization.

In contrast, a single agency offering all services to all clients (single problem and multiple problem) would have only a single board. Under these circumstances it could become difficult to have client representatives for each of the different kinds of clients. Instead, there would probably be representation of the general client population. Such representation could lead to less advocacy for specific client populations, but this need not be the outcome as long as specific advocacy groups still function outside the organization as well as through their representatives on the board. Further, the tenure of board members could be short enough to have membership circulate among different client groups.

Other characteristics. Most of our attention thus far has been devoted to coordination of clients, programs, and resources. We have chosen to emphasize these concepts because we feel they are critical in any service delivery system. However, two other properties—accountability and accessibility—are also important ones to consider in setting up a coordinated system.

Accessibility involves locating services throughout a large metropolitan area and particularly in areas where there is the most use. The intensive study of mental retardation in Los Angeles indicated that most services were located in middle-class areas and most clients were in working-class areas. We feel that having client representatives on the community board can resolve the accessibility issue since they are the ones who are most sensitive to it. The creation of a case-coordination unit is also critical for resolving this issue because it assures a fixed point of referral. In many instances, clients with difficulties do not know where to go for help because no one agency assumes responsibility for them. The creation of a fixed referral point is a critical first step in increasing accessibility. Correct sequencing of services, another aspect of case coordination, is the second step. Cost is an implicit issue here. If the service delivery structure has enough political clout to generate funds from reluctant taxpayers, accessibility is quickly attained.

Accountability is also ensured with our proposed structures. One function of case coordinators is to check that clients have indeed received the services purchased. An advantage of the coalition, though not of the comprehensive organization, is that joint programming increases visibility of staff performance, probably the single best check on the quality of service provided. Team teaching has had this impact, and joint programming should operate in a similar fashion. Finally, we have already noted that the community board in both models increases accountability, at least in its allocation of scarce resources.

For providing accountability the composition of the community board is critical. While in theory it might be desirable to have this board composed entirely of representatives of clients, in practice they do not necessarily do the right thing for clients, as we saw in Bridgeport. The crux of the problem of accountability is that most interest groups are likely to pursue objectives or values in a somewhat single-minded way. The solution is a combination of relevant interest groups as in our community board.

Perhaps even more important than the question of which values are represented is the problem of professional control. Controlling the behavior of professionals and the quality of the service they provide is best done through mechanisms other than a board, even one with professionals on it. Boards lack detailed information about quality service. Heads of organizations always report that they provide quality service, and it is hard to prove otherwise. Professionals on a board protect the interests of their colleagues. However, in our second structure the case-coordination unit and the organizational coalition would increase the amount of professional control through the mechanisms of case coordination and joint programming. Joint programming involves high visibility of professional work to experts who are in the best position to judge quality. Within the organizational coalition, there would be rapid diffusion of knowledge about poor quality work. Since agency members do worry about what other agencies think of their work, such visibility would be a major part of a control process.

Besides creating visibility, keeping professionals abreast of current technological developments helps in controlling the quality of their work. A coalition of organizations is the best structural arrangement for dissemination of new procedures, new standards, and new techniques. By pooling staff in interdependent task situations, one is increasing their learning opportunities, which in turn should result in higher quality care (Hage, 1974). The openness provided in this coalition of organizations may also facilitate technological breakthroughs because of opportunities for the cross-fertilization of ideas.

It would not be wise to rely totally upon interaction among professionals in highly visible and interdependent situations as the sole source of control however. Case coordination is another important structural element. Case coordinators can monitor what is done and then relay this information to the appropriate agencies.

In summary, the major concerns in accountability are the values or interests represented and professional control. We have suggested that a community board, while good for ensuring responsiveness, is not necessarily an effective mechanism for gaining control over the quality of work performed. This control is best achieved by the two other elements in our structure —a case-coordination unit and a coalition of organizations.

An alternative structure. Another approach that we feel has much to recommend it is the creation of a single organization that does nothing but case coordination. All clients would go to fixed points of referral that could be conveniently located in various neighborhood centers. This structure would provide client coordination if not coordination of programs and resources and would go a long way toward solving the problems of accessibility and accountability.

County welfare departments have been providing such coordination to some extent, and we presently have a model also in the district offices of vocational rehabilitation. Indeed, if the federal government were interested in ensuring client coordination, they have the beginnings in the vocational rehabilitation offices. To ensure the participation of private agencies, the government could agree to pay the cost of intake workers if they worked cooperatively in outreach programs with other case coordinators.

For specific kinds of clients such as the mentally retarded, case coordination as a mechanism of change is relatively available to a large number of organizations, both public and private. Indeed, client interest groups such as parents groups could usefully spend their money on this service since it meets one of the most pressing needs and provides them with information about program needs. It also could provide them with greater insight into the problems of agency treatment, although without purchase of services they would not necessarily have much leverage.

Change Strategy

How can this idealized coordination structure be achieved? As in the first chapter, we discuss the change process here as a series of stages. As we have already noted, at least for the field of mental retardation, the awareness stage was already largely achieved by 1962 with the report of the President's Panel. Therefore we do not discuss strategies for creating awareness here but rather assume that the process of change has advanced at least to the point of initiation of a delivery system.

Two other alternatives were suggested in the last chapter, a single organization to provide all services needed to a multi-problem client and a single organization to provide all services to all clients. Neither of these alternatives appears to be politically feasible in the United States at this time. Where such efforts have been attempted (in California and Wisconsin), they have met with great political resistance from existing agencies. No agency wants to be closed or have its authority undermined. One need only briefly consider the number of different groups that would have to be dealt with to bring about these alternatives for service delivery to understand how politically difficult they are: school boards, hospital boards, professional societies, organizational administrators, community chests, and so forth. As a consequence, we do not discuss here strategies for creating these delivery systems; however, we do consider the possibility of combining all case coordination in a single authority structure, perhaps conveniently located in neighborhood centers. That is, we discuss the political problems of how to create a totally integrated case-management organization that does not provide any other services.

Initiation stage. The projects in Milwaukee, Los Angeles, and Cleveland used three different approaches to initiation, and each is instructive. In Milwaukee, a single executive director was largely instrumental in getting the other organizations involved in the AIDS project. This is a particularly interesting example of how the possibility of joint funding can cause organizations to band together, overriding even the suspicion of the motives of this executive director by other directors in the community. Los Angeles organized a group of agencies through a demonstration of need by a large number of professionals; but, despite this step, the possibility of additional funding provided the needed inducement. The Cleveland project demonstrates techniques for creating a community board.

What are the inducements for organizations to participate in a coalition, especially when there will be conflict (Hall and Clark, 1974)? Obviously, funding is a key incentive. The representation of all interest groups on the community board should result in gaining larger taxes if needed for the new delivery system. Although not all organizations that have services for the multiproblem client would necessarily participate (and if they did become involved, they may not be active), if the coalition could raise large sums of money, recalcitrant organizations would be likely to want to participate. Once the power base is big enough, funding is likely to be forthcoming. One of the main advantages of this structure is that it involves so many different interest groups that it is likely to attract political support. We saw what parents groups can do for the mentally retarded in the Bridgeport project. If these interests are combined with elites and professionals and the service delivery organizations are involved as well, then a large and diverse coalition has been established that legislators might find hard to resist, and one can add to this the assumption that the need is real.

A coalition thus provides a new source of funding that leaves previous sources undisturbed. But one should not assume that funding comes first. It did not in Milwaukee. Indeed here we have a particularly compelling case for arguing the efficacy of the coalition because it was formed in the light of considerable conflict between some of the organizations and before there was any guarantee of funding.

Cooperation also results when there is consensus about the interdependence of services (Litwak, 1969). This is a form of domain consensus (Levine and White, 1961; Aldrich, 1972), although it is used somewhat differently here. In other words, there is consensus about the need for a delivery system to manage the interdependent services, even if there is not always consensus about the particular contributions of specific organizations. The needs of the multiproblem client are likely to be beyond those any one organization can fulfill. Also, client needs are best met if they are handled simultaneously in joint programs, rather than piecemeal in a sequential or chain fashion. These needs provide a sustained basis for entering into an exchange because they can be met without threatening the autonomy of organizations. A coalition of organizations can meet these needs but leave agency identities undisturbed. Something is added rather than subtracted or rearranged, and thus the usual reluctance of organizations to enter into mergers or centralized arrangements is overcome.

A hidden benefit is the gain in power, in the capacity to make decisions. Coalitions of organizations can fight far more effectively than a single organization, even a large one. The members of an organizational coalition are likely to have many contacts with influential people in the community, the state, and the nation. Thus, there is the potential for growth in the capacity to mobilize power.

The possibility for self-coordination as opposed to central planning may in itself be a major inducement for participation since such an arrangement allows an agency to contribute to joint decision making and also to set checks on the power of other organizations. Agencies can prevent domination by a single organization because they retain their traditional sources of funds rather than becoming dependent on a fixed point of funding as occurred in each of the five demonstration projects. Thus, organizations may perhaps lose some autonomy, but they gain power in the larger environment. They not only have more funds to allocate, but are free from controls that may interfere with the objectives of the coalition of organizations.

What are the costs involved? An obvious one is that there will be some conflict in the organizational coalition. Having competitors work together involves strains. Research (Hall and

Clark, 1974) suggests that there is more conflict in cooperative relationships than had been previously realized. Work on joint programming (Aiken and Hage, 1968) also indicates that internal coordination problems are created by interorganizational relationships. The needs for more resources make organizations tolerant of this conflict, and the necessity for task interdependence in joint programs can make the bond even stronger. There is also some surrender of autonomy, but, as we suggest above, the gains in power to control the external environment more than offset the losses of autonomy.

Therefore, in sum, this proposal maximizes organizational benefits and minimizes organizational costs. However, it is a proposal that is useful only when there is a relatively clear functional necessity—the need to create a delivery system of organizations—and a technological imperative—the need to work jointly in providing services for the consumer. The minimizing of costs is true for the coalition of organizations designed to meet the needs of a single kind of multiproblem client. It does not appear to be applicable to a coalition of organizations designed to meet the needs of all clients. Here costs would outweigh the benefits.

At this point it is worth discussing the strategy of the federal government to start change processes through demonstration grants. Through the five projects, we became convinced that giving funds to a single organization in a community, except in small cities like Bridgeport, sets into play forces that often preclude the development of a continuum of care for the mentally retarded. This is one of our reasons for arguing that a more appropriate strategy would be to fund a coalition of organizations. In addition, in most cases the amounts of these demonstration grants were too small to accomplish much. Although San Francisco and Bridgeport had more money than they could easily manage, there was still not enough to make it worthwhile for other organizations to participate. Los Angeles got additional funds and found that with these new sources of funding organizations were willing to create the programs. Therefore, a key recommendation is that governments fund delivery systems in sufficiently large amounts to make participation worthwhile. But above all else government agencies interested in stimulating the creation of delivery systems should fund a coalition of private and public agencies and especially a coalition that includes competitors. This precondition for funding can be a major stimulant for the creation of coordinated delivery systems. Requirements for a community board and for a special unit to do case coordination are perhaps less crucial but could be included as well.

In this connection, the creation of a single delivery system for a particular kind of multiproblem client—for example, the aged or the mentally retarded—should stimulate coordination in general. Since a diverse set of organizations is involved, this delivery system opens new channels of communication that can have an impact far beyond the immediate question of the particular kind of client and his needs.

Implementation stage. If there are enough funds and these funds are given to a community board and a coalition of organizations, then we should have many of the preconditions set for the creation of a number of new programs as well as joint programs. Much of our previous research (Aiken and Hage, 1968) as well as some presently unpublished material indicates that the push toward joint programming is great in complex health and welfare agencies. Once the opportunity for additional funding and the structure for joint decision making among the executive directors are created, the probability of even more joint programming is great. Although the dynamics of the decision-making process among executive directors is always hard to predict, it seems reasonable that each agency head will want to maximize his own organizational gains and augment his own area of expertise, and therefore the tendency toward task interdependence will also be great.

Future research will have to evaluate whether a coordinated delivery system leads to higher quality care and better rehabilitation, but on the surface it appears to be an appropriate way of ensuring that the client is treated as a whole person and that fragmentation of care is avoided. Throughout we have focused our attention on the creation of a delivery system, assuming as has everyone else that, in fact, it does provide better care. We need to study the consequences of the various arrangements discussed for the quality of service.

The typical pattern of decision-making regarding innovations within an organization is for one department to propose a new program and for other departments to make suggestions and modifications and often to resist the innovation. Unfortunately, there have not been many studies of resistance to change (for some exceptions see Mann and Williams, 1960; Zaltman, Duncan, and Hollbek, 1973; Hage, 1974). But one established finding is that if those affected by the change are allowed to participate in planning or implementation, their resistance decreases (Selznik, 1949; Coch and French, 1948). The inter-organizational coalition should make easier the process of implementing changes. And because client representatives also are affected by changes, their participation on the coalition committee should increase their acceptance.

But change generally produces resistance, and the creation of new roles in joint programming and the alteration of existing ones will be difficult. We do not want to minimize the problems involved here. Joint funding procedures should be the carrot that ensures continued participation of agencies even when changes seem difficult and threatening to their autonomy.

Routinization stage. If we have correctly identified the elements that are essential in a structure that is designed to achieve coordination of clients, of programs, and of funding, along with accountability and accessibility, and if we have stipulated the major causes of resistance and provided solutions to them, then there should be no problem of survival. A structure that can generate its own power and secure adequate funding is well along the road to institutionalization.

Likewise, we would expect the rapid institutionalization of case management for all clients because there are partial models already, and this appears to be a logical next step. In some respects this may be the easier change to accomplish because the concept of case management is more familiar than the concept of a coalition of organizations with a board.

In conclusion, the key assumption of our argument here is perhaps as old as politics itself, namely, if one wants to achieve a goal that has implications for a set of actors, then one should devise a strategy that somehow either incorporates all interests or accommodates them. This strategy is complicated by the need to include four different elements in a service delivery system, each of which needs to be coordinated in a different way. We have therefore suggested that a rather complex structure is necessary if the goal is indeed coordination of resources, programs, clients, and information for a target group of multiple-handicap clients.

Bibliography

Adrian, C. R. "Some General Characteristics of Nonpartisan Elections." *American Political Science Review,* Sept. 1952, *46,* 766-776.

Aiken, M., and Hage, J. "Organizational Interdependence and Intra-Organizational Structure." *American Sociological Review,* Dec. 1968, *33,* 912-930.

Aiken, M., and Hage, J. "Organizational Permeability, Boundary Spanners and Organizational Structures." Paper read at the American Sociological Association meetings, New Orleans, 1972.

Aldrich, B. C. "Relations Between Organizations: A Critical Review of the Literature." Paper presented at the annual meetings of the American Sociological Association, Washington, D.C., 1970.

Aldrich, H. "An Organizational-Environment Perspective on Cooperation and Conflict Between Organizations in the Manpower and Training System." In A. R. Negandhi (Ed.), *Conflict and Power in Complex Organizations: An Inter-Institutional Perspective.* Kent, Ohio: Comparative Administration Research Institute, College of Business Administration, Kent State University, 1972.

Aldrich, H. "Technology and Organizational Structure: A Re-Examination of the Findings of the Aston Group." *Administrative Science Quarterly*, Mar. 1973, *17*, 26-43.

Aldrich, H. E. "Organizational Boundaries and Inter-Organizational Conflict." *Human Relations*, Aug. 1971, *24*, 279-293.

Alford, R. R. "The Political Economy of Health Care: Dynamics Without Change." *Politics and Society*, 1972, *2*, 127-164.

Alford, R. R. *Health Care Politics: Ideological and Interest Barriers to Reform.* Chicago: University of Chicago Press, 1974.

Alford, R. R., and Lee, E. C. "Voting Turnout in American Cities." *American Political Science Review*, Sept. 1968, *62*, 796-813.

Azumi, K. "Environmental Needs, Resources, and Agents." In K. Azumi and J. Hage (Eds.), *Organizational Systems: A Text-Reader in the Sociology of Organizations.* Lexington, Mass.: Heath, 1972.

Babcock, R. F. *The Zoning Game.* Madison: University of Wisconsin Press, 1969.

Baker, J. H. *Urban Politics in America.* New York: Scribner's, 1971.

Banfield, E. C., and Wilson, J. Q. *City Politics.* Cambridge, Mass.: Harvard University Press, 1965.

Barton, A., and Lazarsfeld, P. F. "Some Functions of Qualitative Analysis in Social Research." *Sociologica*, 1955, *1*, 321-361.

Becker, H. S., and Geer, B. "Participant Observation and Interviewing: A Comparison." *Human Organization*, Fall 1957, *16*, 28-32.

Bloom, T. "Casework Methods Used at Information and Referral Service for the Mentally Retarded." San Francisco, 1968.

Boettcher, R. E. "The 'Service Delivery System': What Is It?" *Public Welfare*, Winter 1974, *32*, 45-50.

Bollens, J. C., and Schmandt, H. J. *The Metropolis: Its People, Politics, and Economic Life.* New York: Harper and Row, 1965.

Buckman, R. O. (Ed.) *Blueprint for the Seventies.* Cleveland: Welfare Federation, 1971a.

Buckman, R. O. *Building a Method of Services, 1963-1967.* Cleveland: Welfare Federation, 1971b.

Buckman, R. O. *Building a Network of Services, 1963-1971.* Cleveland: Welfare Federation of Cleveland, 1971c.

Buttrick, S. M. "On Choice and Services." *Social Service Review,* Dec. 1970, *44,* 427-433.

Buttrick, S. M. "Present Shock. The Future of the Social Services." *Public Welfare,* Fall 1973, *31,* 41-66.

California Legislature. *A Report to: The Assembly Select Committee on Mentally Ill and Handicapped Children. Part I: Services for the Handicapped; Part II: Mentally Disordered Children.* Sacramento, 1970.

California Legislature, Assembly Office of Research. *A Proposal to Reorganize California's Fragmented System of Services for the Mentally Retarded.* Sacramento, 1969.

California Legislature, Assembly Ways and Means Committee, Subcommittee on Mental Health Services. *A Redefinition of State Responsibility for California's Mentally Retarded.* Sacramento, 1965.

California Study Commission on Mental Retardation. *The Undeveloped Resource.* Sacramento, 1965.

Chandler, A. D., Jr. *Strategy and Structure: Chapters in the History of the Industrial Enterprise.* Cambridge, Mass.: MIT Press, 1962.

Coch, L., and French, J., Jr. "Overcoming Resistance to Change." *Human Relations,* Aug. 1948, *1,* 512-532.

Connery, R. H., and others. *The Politics of Mental Health.* New York: Columbia University Press, 1968.

Coser, L. *The Functions of Social Conflict.* New York: Free Press, 1956.

Cumming, E. *Systems of Social Regulation.* New York: Atherton, 1968.

Dill, W. R. "Environment as an Influence on Managerial Autonomy." *Administrative Science Quarterly,* Mar. 1958, *2,* 409-443.

Duff, R., and Hollingshead, A. *Sickness and Society.* New York: Harper and Row, 1968.

Dunham, A. *The New Community Organization.* New York: Crowell, 1970.

Dunn, L. M. *Exceptional Children in the Schools.* (2nd ed.) New York: Holt, Rinehart, and Winston, 1973.

Durkheim, E. *The Division of Labor in Society.* New York: Free Press, 1933.

Elazar, D. J. *American Federalism: A View from the States.* New York: Crowell, 1972.

Eling, R. H. "The Hospital Support Game in Urban Centers." In E. Freidson (Ed.), *The Hospital in Modern Society.* London: Free Press of Glencoe, 1963.

Etzioni, A. *Modern Organizations.* Englewood Cliffs, N.J.: Prentice-Hall, 1964.

Evan, W. "The Organizational Set: Toward a Theory of Inter-organizational Relations." In J. D. Thompson (Ed.), *Approaches to Organizational Design.* Pittsburgh: University of Pittsburgh Press, 1966.

Freidson, E. "Disability as Social Deviance." In M. B. Sussman (Ed.), *Sociology and Rehabilitation.* Washington, D.C.: American Sociological Association, 1966.

Fried, M. "Social Differences in Mental Health." In J. Kosa (Ed.), *Poverty and Health: A Sociological Analysis.* Cambridge, Mass.: Harvard University Press, 1969.

Gilbert, G. R. *Toward a Classification of Social Service Systems: A Theoretical Framework.* Los Angeles: School of Social Work, University of Southern California, 1971.

Gilbert, N. "Assessing Service Delivery Methods: Some Unsettled Questions." *Welfare in Review,* May-June 1972, *10,* 25-33.

Greater Cleveland Mental Retardation Planning Project. *The Mental Retardation Blueprint for Action.* Cleveland: Welfare Federation, 1965.

Greenberg, I. R., and Rodberg, M. L. "The Role of Pre-Paid Group Practice in Relieving the Medical Care Crisis." *Harvard Law Review,* Feb. 1971, *84,* 889-996.

Greenly, J., and Kirk, S. A. "Organizational Characteristics of Agencies and the Distribution of Services to Applicants." *Journal of Health and Human Behavior,* Mar. 1973, *14,* 70-79.

Guetzkow, H. "Relations Among Organizations." In R. V. Bowers (Ed.), *Studies on Behavior in Organizations*. Athens: University of Georgia Press, 1966.

Hage, J. *Communication and Organizational Control: Cybernetics in Health and Welfare Settings*. New York: Wiley, 1974.

Hage, J., and Aiken, M. "Program Change and Organization Properties: A Comparative Analysis." *American Journal of Sociology*, Mar. 1967, *72*, 503-519.

Hage, J., and Aiken, M. *Social Change in Complex Organizations*. New York: Random House, 1970.

Hall, R., and Clark, J. P. "Problems in the Study of Interorganizational Relationships." *Organization and Administrative Sciences*, Spring 1974, *5*, 45-66.

Hall, R. H. "Professionalization and Bureaucratization." *American Sociological Review*, Feb. 1968, *33*, 92-104.

Harrison, P. M. *Authority and Power in the Free Church Tradition*. Princeton, N.J.: Princeton University Press, 1959.

Haurek, E., and Clark, J. P. "Variants of Integration of Social Control Agencies." *Social Problems*, Summer 1967, *15*, 46-59.

Heydebrand, W. "The Study of Organizations." In W. Heydebrand (Ed.), *Comparative Organizations*. Englewood Cliffs, N.J.: Prentice-Hall, 1973.

Hobbs, N. *The Futures of Children: Categories, Labels, and Their Consequences*. San Francisco: Jossey-Bass, 1975.

Hobbs, N. (Ed.) *Issues in the Classification of Children: A Sourcebook on Categories, Labels, and Their Consequences*. San Francisco: Jossey-Bass, 1975.

Hofstadter, R. *The Age of Reform*. New York: Knopf, 1955.

Hollister, C. D. "Interorganizational Conflict: The Case of Police Youth Bureaus and the Juvenile Court." Paper presented at the annual meeting of the American Sociological Association, Washington, D.C., 1970.

Hoshino, G. "Britain's Debate on Universal or Selective Social Services: Lessons for America." *The Social Service Review*, Sept. 1969, *43*, 245-258.

Hurley, R. *Poverty and Mental Retardation: A Causal Relationship*. New York: Random House, 1969.

Kahn, A. J. "Perspectives on Access to Social Services." *Social Work*, Apr. 1970, *15*, 95-102.

Kahn, F. J. "Public Social Services: The Next Phase—Policy and Delivery Strategies." *Public Welfare*, Winter 1972, *30*, 15-24.

Kanner, L. *A History of the Care and Study of the Mentally Retarded.* Springfield, Ill.: Thomas, 1964.

Koogan, G. E., Rogers, D. L., and Paulson, S. K. "Measurement of Interorganizational Relations: A Deterministic Model." Paper presented at the annual meeting of the American Sociological Association, New Orleans, 1972.

Kronick, J. C., Perlmutter, F. D., and Gummer, B. "The APWA Model Social Service Delivery System: A Preliminary Assessment." *Public Welfare*, Fall 1973, *31*, 47-53.

Landau, M. "Redundancy, Rationality, and the Problem of Duplication and Overlap." *Public Administration Review*, July 1969, *29*, 346-358.

Lawrence, P. R., and Lorsch, J. W. *Organization and Environment: Managing Differentiation and Integration.* Boston: Harvard Business School, 1967.

Lazarsfeld, P., and Menzel, H. "On the Relation Between Individual and Collective Properties." In A. Etzioni (Ed.), *A Sociological Reader on Complex Organizations.* New York: Holt, Rinehart, and Winston, 1969.

Lee, E. C. *The Politics of Nonpartisanship.* Berkeley: University of California Press, 1960.

Lees, E. "An Example of a One-Stop Center for Referral of the Mentally Retarded." San Francisco, 1968.

Lefton, M. "Client Characteristics and Structural Outcomes: Toward the Specification of Linkages." In W. Rosengren and M. Lefton (Eds.), *Organizations and Clients: Essays in the Sociology of Science.* Columbus, Ohio: Merrill, 1970.

Lefton, M. "Client Characteristics and Organizational Functioning: Interorganizational Focus." In A. R. Negandhi (Ed.), *Organization Theory in an Interorganizational Perspective.* Kent, Ohio: Comparative Administration Research Institute, College of Business Administration, Kent State University, 1971.

Lefton, M., and Rosengren, W. R. "Organizations and Clients: Lateral and Longitudinal Dimensions." *American Sociological Review,* Dec. 1966, *31,* 802-810.

Levine, S., and White, P. E. "Exchange as a Conceptual Framework for the Study of Interorganizational Relationships." *Administrative Science Quarterly,* Mar. 1961, *5,* 583-601.

Likert, R. *The Human Organization.* New York: McGraw-Hill, 1967.

Litwak, E. "Models of Bureaucracy Which Permit Conflict." *American Journal of Sociology,* Sept. 1961, *67,* 177-184.

Litwak, E. *Towards the Theory and Practice of Coordination Between Formal Organizations.* Ann Arbor: School of Social Work, University of Michigan, 1969.

Litwak, E. *Towards the Multi-Factor Theory and Practices of Linkages Between Formal Organizations.* CRD-425-C2-9. Washington, D.C.: Department of Health, Education, and Welfare, 1970.

Litwak, E., and Hylton, L. F. "Interorganizational Analysis, A Hypothesis on Coordinating Agencies." *Administrative Science Quarterly,* Mar. 1962, *6,* 395-420.

Litwak, E., and Meyer, H. "Towards a Multi-Factor Theory and Practice of Linkages Between Formal Organizations." ORD-425-CL-9. Washington, D.C.: Department of Health, Education, and Welfare, 1970.

Litwak, E., and Rothman, J. "Towards the Theory and Practice of Coordination Between Formal Organizations." In W. Rosengren and M. Lefton (Eds.), *Organizations and Clients: Essays in the Sociology of Science.* Columbus, Ohio: Merrill, 1970.

Lynch, M. "The Physician 'Shortage,' The Economists' Mirror." *The Annals of the American Academy of Political and Social Sciences,* Jan. 1972, *399,* 82-88.

Mann, F., and Williams, L. "Observations on the Dynamics of a Change to Electronic Data Processing Equipment." *Administrative Science Quarterly,* Sept. 1960, *5,* 217-257.

March, J., and Simon, H. *Organizations.* New York: Wiley, 1958.

March, M. S. "The Neighborhood Concept." *Public Welfare,* Apr. 1968, *26,* 97-111.

Mayer, R. R. "Social Change or Service Delivery?" In *Social Welfare Forum: Official Proceedings. National Conference on Social Welfare.* New York: Columbia University Press, 1970.

Mental Retardation Area Board V. *Areawide Mental Retardation Plan.* San Francisco, 1971.

Mental Retardation Program Board of Los Angeles County. *Plan for Mental Retardation Services, Area 10.* Los Angeles, 1972.

Mental Retardation Services Board of Los Angeles County. *Report of Activities.* Los Angeles, 1968.

Michels, R. *Political Parties.* New York: Free Press, 1949.

Miller, D. "The Language of Systems Analysis (Systems Analysis: Phase One; Systems Analysis: Phase Two)." San Francisco: San Francisco Coordinating Council on Mental Retardation, 1967.

Miller, D., and Tallenbaum, R. "1964 Census of Known Retarded." San Francisco Coordinating Council on Mental Retardation, 1964.

Miller, W. B. "Inter-Institutional Conflict as a Major Impediment to Delinquency Prevention." *Human Organization,* 1958, *17*(3), 20-23.

Milwaukee County Mental Health-Mental Retardation Planning Committee. *Guidelines for Mental Health-Mental Retardation Planning.* Milwaukee, 1965.

Morris, R. "Welfare Reform 1973: The Social Services Dimension." *Science,* Aug. 1973, *181,* 515-522.

Mott, B. "Coordination and Interorganizational Relations in Health." In P. E. White and G. Vlasak (Eds.), *Interorganizational Research in Health.* Baltimore: Johns Hopkins Press, 1970.

Negandhi, A. (Ed.) *Conflict and Power in Complex Organizations: An Inter-Institutional Perspective.* Kent, Ohio: Comparative Administration Research Institute, College of Business Administration, Kent State University, 1972.

Netzger, D. *Economics and Urban Problems: Diagnoses and Prescriptions.* (2nd ed.) New York: Basic Books, 1974.

Newton, K. "A Critique of the Pluralist Model." *Acta Sociologica,* 1969, *12,* 209-223.

O'Donnell, E. J., and Reid, O. M. "The Multiservice Neighborhood Center. Neighborhood Challenge and Center Response." *Welfare in Review,* May-June 1972, *10,* 1-19.

O'Donnell, E. J., and Sullivan, M. M. "Service Delivery and Social Action Through the Neighborhood Center: A Review of Research." *Welfare in Review,* Nov.-Dec. 1969, *7,* 1-13.

Olson, M., Jr. *The Logic of Collective Action, Public Goods and the Theory of Groups.* New York: Schocken, 1968.

Orzack, L., Charland, B. H., and Halliday, H. *The Pursuit of Change Series.* Bridgeport, Conn.: Parents and Friends of Mentally Retarded Children in Bridgeport, 1969.

Parsons, T. *The Social System.* New York: Free Press, 1951.

Perrow, C. "Hospitals: Technology, Structure, and Goals." In J. March (Ed.), *Handbook of Organizations.* Chicago: Rand McNally, 1965.

Perrow, C. "A Framework for the Comparative Analysis of Organizations." *American Sociological Review,* Apr. 1967, *32,* 194-208.

President's Panel on Mental Retardation. *National Action to Combat Mental Retardation.* Washington, D.C., 1962.

Reid, W. "Interagency Coordination in Delinquency Prevention and Control." *Social Science Review,* Dec. 1964, *38,* 418-428.

Reid, W. "Interorganizational Cooperation: A Review and Critique of Current Theory." In P. E. White and G. Vlasak (Eds.), *Interorganizational Research in Health.* Baltimore: Johns Hopkins Press, 1970.

Rosengren, W. "The Careers of Clients and Organizations." In W. Rosengren and M. Lefton (Eds.), *Organizations and Clients: Essays in the Sociology of Science.* Columbus, Ohio: Merrill, 1970.

Rosengren, W., and Lefton, M. *Hospitals and Patients.* New York: Atherton, 1969.

Rosengren, W., and Lefton, M. (Eds.) *Organizations and Clients: Essays in the Sociology of Science.* Columbus, Ohio: Merrill, 1970.

Safilios-Rothschild, C. *The Sociology and Social Psychology of Disability and Rehabilitation.* New York: Random House, 1970.

San Francisco Coordinating Council on Mental Retardation. *Progress Reports for RD-1929-G: Grant Proposal, 1965; Pilot Study, 1965*. San Francisco, 1966, 1968.

San Francisco Coordinating Council on Mental Retardation. *Final Report—Community Organization Action Plan for the Mentally Retarded*. San Francisco, 1970.

San Francisco Coordinating Council on Mental Retardation. *San Francisco County Mental Retardation Plan for AB 225*. San Francisco, 1971.

Schnore, L. F. *The Urban Scene*. New York: Free Press, 1965.

Schoff, G. H. *A Structured Community Approach to Complete Services for the Retarded*. Milwaukee: Jewish Vocational Services of Milwaukee, 1970.

Scott, R. A. *The Making of Blind Men*. New York: Russell Sage Foundation, 1969.

Scott, W. R. "Field Methods in the Study of Organizations." In J. G. March (Ed.), *Handbook of Organizations*. Chicago: Rand McNally, 1965.

Seeley, J. R., and others. *Community Chest: A Case Study in Philanthropy*. Toronto: University of Toronto Press, 1957.

Selznik, P. *T.V.A. and the Grass Roots: A Study in the Sociology of Formal Organizations*. Berkeley: University of California Press, 1949.

Sharpe, L. J. "American Democracy Reconsidered." *British Journal of Political Science*, 1973, *3*, 1-28, 129-168.

Shils, E. A., and Finch, H. A. *Max Weber on the Methodology of the Social Sciences*. New York: Free Press, 1949.

Shonfield, A. *Modern Capitalism, The Changing Balance of Public and Private Power*. London: Oxford University Press, 1969.

Sills, D. *The Volunteers: Means and Ends in a National Organization*. New York: Free Press, 1957.

Somers, A. R. (Ed.) *The Kaiser-Permanente Medical Care Program*. Proceedings of a symposium, Oakland, Calif., 1971.

Somers, H. M., and Somers, A. R. *Doctors, Patients, and Health Insurance*. Washington, D.C.: Brookings Institution, 1961.

Stein, M. *The Eclipse of Community: An Interpretation of American Studies.* Princeton, N.J.: Princeton University Press, 1960.

Terryberry, S. "The Evolution of Organizational Environments." *Administrative Science Quarterly,* Mar. 1968, *12,* 590-613.

Thompson, J. D. *Organizations in Action.* New York: McGraw-Hill, 1967.

Turk, H. "Comparative Urban Structure from an Interorganizational Perspective." *Administrative Science Quarterly,* Mar. 1973, *18,* 37-55.

Vidich, A. J., and Bensman, J. *Small Town in Mass Society.* Princeton, N.J.: Princeton University Press, 1958.

Walton, J. "The Vertical Axis of Community Organizations and the Structure of Community Power." *Southwestern Social Science Quarterly,* Dec. 1962, *48,* 353-368.

Warren, R. "Alternative Strategies of Inter-Agency Planning." In P. E. White and G. Vlasak (Eds.), *Interorganizational Research in Health.* Baltimore: Johns Hopkins Press, 1970.

Warren, R. *Truth, Love, and Social Change, and Other Essays on Community Change.* Chicago: Rand McNally, 1971.

Warren, R. L. "The Interorganizational Field as a Focus for Investigation." *Administrative Science Quarterly,* Dec. 1967, *12,* 396-419.

Warren, R. L. *The Community in America.* (2nd ed.) Chicago: Rand McNally, 1972.

Warren, R. L., Rose, S. M., and Bergunder, A. F. *The Structure of Urban Reform.* Lexington, Mass.: Heath, 1974.

White, P. "Exchange as a Conceptual Framework for Understanding Interorganizational Relationships: Applications to Non-Profit Organizations." In A. R. Negandhi (Ed.), *Organization Theory in an Interorganizational Perspective.* Kent, Ohio: Comparative Administration Research Institute, College of Business Administration, Kent State University, 1971.

White, P., and Vlasak, G. (Eds.) *Interorganizational Research in Health.* Washington, D.C.: Public Health Services, National Center for Health Services and Research Development, Department of Health, Education, and Welfare, 1970.

Wolfensberger, W., and Kurtz, R. A. (Eds.) *Management of the Family of the Mentally Retarded.* Chicago: Follett, 1969.

Yuchtman, E., and Seashore, S. E. "A System Approach to Organizational Effectiveness." *American Sociological Review,* Dec. 1967, *32,* 891-903.

Zaltman, G., Duncan, R., and Hollbek, J. *Innovations and Organizations.* New York: Wiley, 1973.

Zeitz, G. "Interorganizational Relationships and Social Structure: A Critique of Some Aspects of the Literature." *Organization and Administrative Sciences,* Spring 1974, *5,* 131-140.

Index